SELLC

M000317778

SELLOSOPHY

THE ART AND SCIENCE BEHIND B2B SALES AND BUSINESS DEVELOPMENT

Ariel Feder

Dedication

To the sagest person I know, my daughter Keila.
To the most self-assured person I know,
my daughter Nessa.
When I will be fully-fledged,
I hope to be like you.

To love of my life, my beautiful Jane, who combines both of
those personal qualities in her character.

Table of Contents

Introduction

Dear Reader,
Thank you for picking up this book. I know you are very busy and have plenty of things to do. I will quickly reveal what this book is all about, so you won't waste your time if it's not for you.

If you are looking for a broader and a more fundamental view on sales management, this is the book for you. I wrote it especially for professionals such as you--corporate managers and leaders, business developers, business owners, sales managers, distributions managers and sales professionals. The book is for all thinking people who are in business-to-business sales.

I will share with you my approach to establish and manage an outstanding sales organization. You will understand the mechanisms behind salespeople's motivation, partner recruitment and business development. Each chapter dives into a different fundamental aspect of sales management.

This book will challenge your view of sales management. In each chapter, we will create mental models to guide you through the uncertainty of the business world and will provide you with a model to remember long after reading this book. These models combine field experience with the ideas of the greatest philosophers of all time.

In this book, you will not find lists of must-have qualities. You won't learn *the five most important prospecting questions*. You will not find basic sales tactics. You won't memorize scripts for sales calls. You won't find motivation stories to *go and sell now*. While all those things are helpful, they are quickly forgotten. Rather, in this book you'll discover the mechanisms behind effective B2B sales management.

I hope this book will help you build your own intellectual approach and practical philosophy for B2B sales management. A practical philosophy to develop your own vision and keep you on track in times of uncertainty.

> *"If I have seen farther,*
> *it is by standing on the shoulders of Giants."*
> *-Isaac Newton in 1675* [1]

This book integrates the philosophical ideas of great minds into practical models. You will find applications of Victor Frankel's and Yuval Noah Harari's ideas into motivating people. Taoist teachings into developing new markets. The findings of Daniel Kahneman and Dan Ariely lay out the fundamentals of recruitment salespeople processes. The theorems of James Clerk Maxwell and Abraham De Moivre help to define success and expertise. The writings of Nassim Talab and Sir William Francis Butler contribute to sales organization structure models.

Thank you for reading so far. I wrote this book because I had a burning desire to share my ideas with you. I hope this work will contribute to your success. It will be a great privilege for me to know your opinion about the ideas in this book.

Thank you.

I am grateful to James Clerk Maxwell, Abraham De Moivre, Nassim Taleb, Clayton Christensen, Criss Voss, Karl Paul Reinhold Niebuhr, Mike Tyson, Buddha, Karl Popper and Carl von Clausewitz.

I have a great appreciation to ideas of Thomas Gilovich, W. Edwards Deming, Yuval Noah Harari, Napoleon Hill, Brent Adamso, Friedrich Nietzsche, Sun Tzu, Epicurus, Conan Doyle, Nabil Sabio Azadi, Abraham Lincoln and Sir William Francis Butler.

Acknowledgments

I'd like to thank my wife Jane and my daughters Nessa and Keila. Thank you for the time you gave me to write this manuscript. I am sorry that my passion to write this book, robbed us form precious times that could be spent together.

"If I have seen further it is by standing on the shoulders of Giants."
-Isaac Newton in 1675 [1]

Sellosophy integrates philosophical ideas of great minds into practical models. Ideas of outstanding people--philosophers, mathematicians, scientists, historians, generals, intellectuals, spiritual teachers, psychologists, sages and business leaders. To them I am internally grateful for the light they brought into our world.

I am thankful to Tauist Chinese Huinang masters Victor Frankel, Abraham Maslow, Daniel Kahneman and Dan Ariely.

Chapter 1

Business Development and Getting Into New Markets

"When the best generals use arms, they have the way of heaven above, the advantages of earth below and the hearts of men in between. Then they used them at the optimum moment, deploying them along with the momentum of the situation. This is why they have no broken troops or defeated armies. As for the mediocre generals, they do not know the way of heaven above and do not know the advantages of earth. They only use people and momentum.

Although they cannot be completely successful, their victories will be in the majority. When it comes to inferior generals and the way they use arms. They hear a lot but confuse themselves. They know a lot but doubt themselves. They are fearful of camp and hesitant in action. Therefore, they are likely to be captured by others."

The Book of Leadership and Strategy - Lesson of the Chinese Masters. [2]

Getting into new markets is a difficult and risky task. Company investment may not pay off and sales managers will be responsible for this failure. The lack of experience and deficiency of resources will reduce efficiency and performance. Things won't go smoothly.

The logistics support of your company will be much more complicated. The needs of this market may not fit into existing processes. It will affect salespeople and new customers alike.

If the development of a new market is your job, I wish you a stroke of good luck. It won't be easy, but it will be interesting. Perhaps, from time to time, you'll wish you could be responsible for more mature markets with less uncertainty, higher sales volume and more resources. This certainly sounds much better than stepping into the fog of war.

If your mind is wandering in a negative direction, please remind yourself that the development of new business is crucial for your company's survival. The business world is extremely competitive, and if a company doesn't constantly seek new markets, it will perish. As soon as a certain market matures, low-cost competition will enter it and margins will decrease. So, every company must innovate. As competitors enter into our core businesses, we are obliged to enter into other markets. We must find new, more profitable markets and diversify our businesses. We must commercially innovate and get into new markets.

In this chapter, we'll go over the process of defining our offering and finding potential customers. We'll start by understanding our offering, focusing on segmentation and customer selection based on our customer's needs. We will then build a step-by-step model to create a Go-to-Market strategy. The opening quote will assist us to illustrate and remember the concepts of this chapter. This quote is from *The Book of Leadership and Strategy* by Tauist Chinese Huinang Masters.

To start off on the right foot, let's establish a common language. I would like to present the fundamental ideas which are the basis of this model.

Product Knowledge

"When best generals use arms, they have the way of heaven above, the advantages of earth below and the hearts of men in between."

Let suppose that the *way of heaven* is market knowledge and the *advantages of the earth below* is our product. The product is a given, and the market is large and unknown. Before we do anything, we have to know where we stand with our offering, *the earth below*. Without it, we cannot know what customer problems we can solve, so we cannot look for potential customers.

The first step is truly and deeply understanding all the technical and commercial attributes of our products and services. We must know the advantages and limitations of our product. If we aren't firm in this field, we should find someone from R&D to train us. Go over all the success stories and look for patterns. Usually, salespeople say their customers purchased their product because of a great relationship. This is not the whole truth. The product must solve some challenges for customers, or they will not buy it. A relationship is a tool, but it is not the reason for a B2B deal. Look for problems our product solves for the customer.

Knowledge of the product is a must for any sales professional!

Jobs to be Done

Harvard Professor Clayton Christensen introduced in his book *The Innovator's Solution* a theory of *Jobs-to-be- Done*.[3] Clayton's claims that customers are not buying products because they want to have them. Customers are buying because they have a job which needs to be done. Customers are hiring the product for specific jobs. For example, a car, a bus, and the metro subway have almost the same job in our lives, commuting to the office and back. Customers buy dishwashers because they have dishes to wash. Smartphones with HD cameras took away the job of simple photo cameras. Nowadays, people are buying fewer Canon cameras since this job is adequately done with the smartphone. So, in buying, it is not about the ownership of the product but about solving a challenge and doing a job.

R&D develops products to meet a certain specification and a list of attributes. In the high-tech industry, those attributes are called features. R&D people are quite proud of these features. They will tell you their product is faster, smaller, stronger and has more memory. R&D will present the product to you in the same way they planned it—as a list of features according to specifications. R&D managers will emphasize that the product will meet all the customer's requirements. They will tell you that your product has better specs than the competition. At some point, they may list applications for this product. An *application* is basically a high-level description of product usability. Rarely, they'll get into a discussion about specific problems which we can solve for the customer. Mostly, they'll stay on a high level talking about applications.

This may be a good way to introduce a new product internally, but this way of thinking will prevent us from finding new customers for our products. As business developers, we need to turn this upside down. We should start with *Jobs to be Done*. We should seek customer's known and unknown challenges which we can solve with our products. A summary of jobs to be done should be our starting point.

Next, we should talk about all the benefits our product provides the customer by doing those jobs. We should consider the benefits our customers obtained when they chose us over the competition.

Only in the last step should we be focusing on specifications and features. The last step shows us how all the benefits mentioned above are supported by the technical specifications.

This is exactly how we should train our salespeople to present our products to our customers. This is the most efficient way we can convey a message. For example, "Mr. Customer, we know you have this job to do. We can do this job much better than the competition because our product is technologically superior."

Figure 1-1 is a flow chart of the effective marketing and selling messaging processes of our product to customers.

FIGURE 1-1

Flowchart to present products to customers.
Instead of starting from product specifications...

Start with the jobs customers want us to do.

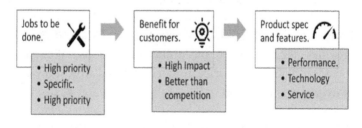

So, for example:

> *XYZ mp3 Player has the following features:* Meets IP65
> standard, Bluetooth, lightweight, robust, works in
> temperatures from 23°f to 113°f, strong grip, 32G of
> memory, fast charging and quality sound.

> *XYZ mp3 Player benefits are:* High-quality music
> underwater and comfortable to swim with. It can store a lot
> of music, and it will not fall from your head. Takes just
> three minutes to charge.

> *XYZ mp3 Player can do the following jobs for us:* Listening
> to music when I run in the snow during winter and when I
> swim in the pool during summer.

Now, let us turn it upside down following the model above:

> *XYZ mp3 Player JOB:* Listening to music while running in
> cold winter and swimming in hot summer.

> *XYZ mp3 Player Benefit:* Comfortable, doesn't fall off, a lot
> of music storage, easy to use, the same product for
> swimming and running.

> *XYZ mp3 Player Features:* Meets IP68 standard
> (waterproof), Bluetooth, 32G of memory, works in
> temperatures from 23°f to 113°f, strong grip, fast charging
> and lightweight.

Many jobs can be supported by the same features. Most of the
jobs don't require every feature of the product. So, for a certain

customer job, many unused features don't provide any benefit to the customer. Thus, we should not focus on those features.

The key thing here is to find jobs our product is good at solving. These jobs may be different from market to market, so as we enter new markets, our former experience may not be relevant. Customers in new markets may use our products differently. They may need us to do jobs that original product definitions could not anticipate. It is our job as business developers to find new jobs for our products in new markets.

According to Freakonomics, Listerine was originally marketed as a floor cleaner and a cure for gonorrhea. Listerine did not become commercially successful until it rebranded as a cure for bad breath. The company's revenues rose from $115,000 to more than $8,000,000 in the seven years after they changed Listerine's job.[4]

A camera in front of the smartphone was designed as a video conferencing camera. In the beginning, the video conference did not support FHD resolution, so smartphones had low-end cameras on the front panels. Suddenly something new happened. In 2013, *selfie* was the word of the year. As you can imagine, in 2013, the low-end front camera was vastly used to take pictures. The next generation of smartphones was adjusted accordingly.

We should not miss business opportunities by misunderstanding customer needs. *Jobs to be Done* is the critical step in any Go-to-Market strategic plan.

Best Go-to-Market plans are based on five-to-seven jobs that our products can do for our customers in the new market which have a high impact on high-priority jobs. In addition, these jobs should be common enough to have a wide customer base in a new market.

We must go out into the field and confirm our hypotheses. We must go out and talk to our customers. We should run our ideas by sales representatives, distributors, managers, and potential users. This is a great investment of our time.

Complexity of Large B2B Deals

One of the main challenges of large B2B deals is extremely long sales cycles which involve a lot of sales and marketing resources. In their book *The Challenger Customer* Brent Adamson and Matthew Dixon described the problematic buying process of B2B customers. [5] Their main point is that the amount of marketing information is beyond human comprehension. Customers are lost in an infinite amount of data. Confused customers tend to avoid making any buying decisions.

At the same time, the average number of decisionmakers in a typical company rose from two to 5.4 people. Needs and solutions have become complex both technically and commercially, so companies must rely on competence of at least five employees to make the decision. In such conditions, people who have to make the purchase decision may not perceive the entire picture. They are not able to process all the available information. This makes the decision process extremely complex. As a result, customers tend to procrastinate in their decisions. Eventually, when they are forced to decide, they fail to consider all the pros and cons of each alternative.

When confused, people tend to agree about one thing everyone understands. *Money.* It is much easier for the six decisionmakers to reach consensus on the lowest offered price, then on technical superiority. Therefore, they may neglect the long-term benefits of your solution and give the project to the lowest price offering. This is bad for everyone concerned. Low prices are bad for the sellers in the short-run and for the customers in the long run. The problem isn't the lack of information or method of decision. The problem is too much information and an overly complex decision process with multiple stakeholders.

How can we overcome this?

We need to provide a customer with a crystal-clear solution. A solution is a combination of several *Jobs to be Done.* As we discussed before, *Jobs to be Done* can be technical, financial, or emotional, so we need to have a wider look than merely solving a specific technical problem. We need to provide a customer with a solution that fits his needs on all levels, addressing the technical, commercial, political and personal needs of involved stakeholder.

We should understand and address all those needs and design an easy decision for engineers, purchasing and managers alike.

The reaction of customer stakeholders to our solution should be, "That's right!" We must remember this concept as it will dramatically shorten our sales cycles.

"That's right!" The customer doesn't need to say, "It's a good product," or "It has better performance," or "Your product is more cost-effective." All of these statements can be flipped over by our competitors at their next meeting. Our competitors may have the same features, or they might reduce the price and we will lose the deal. The feeling our customer must have as we finish the meeting is, "This salesperson understands me and my needs. This is the right solution for my company."

The *That's right!* concept is well depicted in the book *Never Split the Difference* by Chris Voss. [6] This response from a customer basically means, "We understand that you understood us. Your solution reflects your understanding and meets most of our real needs. It isn't perfect, but it is the right solution for us. Since you understand us, we would like to do business with you."

A close friend of mine works as a business development manager for an international electronics company. This company builds equipment for major players in the semiconductor industry. His company recently released a new machine, let's call it Alpha. It was a product with superior performance, features, and a great human interface. The main differentiator was the high sensitivity power input, which is useful in power semiconductor design and manufacturing. Several large competitors dominated this market segment for some time, and customers got used to their products. As my friend promoted Alpha in his territory, his competitors responded with price reductions that were quite effective in the beginning.

Machines for semiconductors are complex and have multiple

advantages and disadvantages. An objective comparison between different machines is extremely time-consuming, so customers prefer to stick to what they already know. In this domain, some engineers have a mantra, "If it works, don't fix it."

In some cases, management and purchasing are pushing engineers to use new technologies. By implementing them, management is trying to reduce cost and improve efficiency. But as the large competitors reduce their prices, management loses interest in innovation. Winning the market from strong competitors who are willing to majorly discount is not an easy task. My friend had to do something different than merely competing on price with the same customers.

Alpha had the unique ability to measure sensitive power signals, an important *Job to be Done* for designers of the power semiconductors. He knew he had a niche.

At first, he mapped all power semiconductor companies who worked with sensitive signals. He learned their *Jobs to be Done* and his competitors' technical gaps. Together with his team, he constructed a solution around this specific *Job to be Done*. It was not just a technical advantage--it was a full solution for customers who experienced those challenges. His solutions included software, accessories, onsite training, short-term loan, rental options, and technical support.

To communicate this solution to customers, he chose the personal approach. He didn't bombard customers with email and calls. Rather, he invited specific customers and their managers for a demonstration. As his application engineers were presenting the unique technical advantages for power semiconductors, he was presenting to high management different ownership models to solve their budget limitations. Then he presented a reasonable transaction plan with training programs and technical support with minimal downtime.

There was no downside for the engineers and no risk for the management. It was an easy decision for all parties involved. An exact fit for all aspects.

One by one, he managed to flip a major portion of his customers. Those major wins established him as a close partner for semiconductor vendors in his territory.

Our discussion about product knowledge, *Jobs to be Done* and B2B deal complexity lays the foundation for the development of the *Go-to-Market Strategy*.

Let us work together and create a *Go-to-Market Strategy* in six steps.

Go-to-Market Strategy for a New Market

"*When the best generals use arms, they have the way of heaven above, the advantages of the earth below and the hearts of men between. Then they used them at the optimum moment, deploying them along with the momentum of the situation. This is why they have no broken troops or defeated armies.*"

STEP 1 – Know your Products
Knowledge of our offering is the first and fundamental step in the life of any sales professional. There is NO excuse for having poor knowledge of our portfolio. Meeting customers without

the ability to articulate our offering is a mistake. Developing strategies without knowing our products will lead to disaster.

STEP 2 - List all Potential Customers

Market knowledge is the knowledge of potential customers in the market. We should invest time and effort in finding, characterizing, and profiling potential customers. It's best to hire a salesperson who knows the new market. We may also hire external agencies and consulting firms which can aid us in this research. Every market has its own dynamics and sources of information, so it's hard to say something general about market research methods. Rather, let us discuss the desired outcome of this research and how we can convert it into sales.

We should make the effort and create a list of customers who will contribute at list 80% of the revenue. If it is a B2B market involving complex and expensive solutions, there should be about 20-30 customers on the list. If it is a more commoditized market, we may have 200 customers on this list.

In the B2C market, it's best to look at groups with the same characteristics. In some literature, these are called *Tribes*. [7] Tribal marketing and B2C sales are outside the specs of this book. In this book, we'll focus on B2B sales.

The outcome of this research should be a table containing customer names and relevant characteristics. These characteristics may include the address of the business, the number of employees, company growth, yearly R&D investment, number of potential users and addressable *Jobs to be Done*. Table 1-1 is a typical example of the outcome of **STEP 1**.

TABLE 1-1

Example of a table of potential customers in the new market. For this example, we will assume our core business is IT solutions for large companies.

	Cutomers	Employees	Company growth	IT Investment	Number of customers	Jobs to be done	Addressable business
1	Alpha	10,000	5%	$50M	300	CRM, Stock, Storage, Database	$7M
2	Beta	10,000	-3%	$40M	250	CRM, Storage	$5M
3	Gamma	10,000	5%	$30M	250	CRM, Storage, Database	$2.5M
4	Delta	5,000	3%	$25M	300	Stock, Database	$2M
5	Epsilon	5,000	-10%	$25M	500	Stock, Database	$0.5M
6	Zeta	5,000	5%	$10M	100	AI	$0.7M
7	Eta	5,000	3%	$15M	200	AI	$1M
8	Theta	1,000	10%	$1M	100	Accounting, Stock, AI, Database	$0.3M
9	Iota	1,000	10%	$1M	50	Accounting, Stock, AI, Database	$0.3M
10	Kappa	1,000	10%	$1.5M	150	Accounting, Stock, AI	$0.3M

STEP 3 - Customer Segments and Solutions

Customizing solutions for 100-200 customers in our new market is an enormous task. We'll probably not have resources to support it. Therefore, we need to create *Customer Segments* and *Customer Segments Solutions.*

In order to find a *Customer Segment*, we will use the customer list from **STEP 2**. We will create a new table (Table 1-2). The colons will represent the *Jobs to be Done* and rows will represent companies. In each cell, we will write a commercial offering: sale, rental, leasing, partnership, service, donation and more. As we populate the table, we'll see a map of our market. Looking at this map, we'll spot *Customer Segments.* Customers in the same segment will have similar *Jobs to be Done* and will have similar commercial offerings.

TABLE 1-2

Example table of commercial offering for different customers with different *Jobs to be Done*.

	Customers	Jobs We Can Do / Jobs to be Down					
		CRM	Accounting Soft	Stock Management	AI Robots	Data Storage	Customers Database
1	Alpha	Sale		Service		Leasing	Sale, Partnership
2	Beta	Sale				Rental, Sale	
3	Gamma	Partnership				Rental, Sale	Partnership
4	Delta			Service			Sale
5	Epsilon			Service			Sale
6	Zeta				Sale		
7	Eta				Partnership		
8	Theta		Sale	Service	Rental		Sale
9	Iota		Sale	Service	Rental		Sale
10	Kappa		Sale	Service	Rental		

Now we can look for *Customer Segments* and mark them on the table. Table 1-3 is one way to do it. In your own analysis, you may use colors and stickers.

TABLE 1-3

Example table of *Customer Segments* based on commercial offering and *Jobs to be Done*.

	Customers	Jobs We Can Do / Jobs to be Done					
		CRM	Accounting Soft	Stock Management	AI Robots	Data Storage	Customers Database
1	Alpha	Sale		Service		Leasing	Sale, Partnership
2	Beta	Sale				Rental, Sale	
3	Gamma	Partnership				Rental, Sale	Partnership
4	Delta			Service			Sale
5	Epsilon			Service			Sale
6	Zeta				Sale		
7	Eta				Partnership		
8	Theta		Sale	Service	Rental		Sale
9	Iota		Sale	Service	Rental		Sale
10	Kappa		Sale	Service	Rental		

Now we are ready for the interesting part!

Let's find a *Customer Segment Solution* for each *Customer Segment*. A solution is a combination of several *Jobs to be Done* and commercial offerings. Based on previous examples, we can create **Table 1-4**.

TABLE 1-4

Example table of *Customer Segments Solutions* based on commercial offering and *Jobs to be Done*.

	Customer Segments	Customer Segment Solution	Products	Sort of Deal	Customer name
1	CRM sales to large corporates	CRM sales with local support	CRM	Sales or Partnership	Alpha, Beta, Gamma
2	Stock management service	Stock management service	Stock	Service contract	Alpha, Delta, Epsilon
3	Small company package	Software for logistics package	AI , Stock, Accounting	Sale, Rental & Service	Theta, Iota, Kappa
4	Storage and Data management	Rental storage and database Management - end to end	Storage & Database Management	Sale & Rental	Alpha, Beta, Gamma, Delta, Epsilon, Theta, Iota

STEP 4 - Deployment of Resources
".... Then they used them at the optimum moment, deploying them along with the momentum of the situation. This is why they have no broken troops or defeated armies."

A major portion of a new market strategy is the deployment of resources. It would be best if we had a dedicated account manager for each customer, but we know that isn't reasonable. In order for our company to be profitable, it has to keep operational costs down.

Finding an efficient and *good enough* way to sell is the key. The set of sales techniques we use is different for each market, industry, and time. We may consider a few of these techniques: face-to-face meetings, on-site seminars, product demonstrations, product evaluations, product trials, video conferences, webinars, telemarketing, dedicated email, promotional events and more. We should also decide if our employees will do those activities, or if we will work with a channel (distribution partners). It comes down to internal versus external resources.

Let us call this combination of sales techniques a *Sales Approach*. In some cases, a *Sales Approach* may mean having a dedicated account manager with deep technical knowledge in addition to an external telemarketing company cold calling prospects. In others, it may totally rely on distribution.

Let's consider a few examples of our *Sales Approach*. If we are selling a spa treatment, a frontal meeting may be too much. Instead, we can work with a telemarketing agency to personally inform potential customers of our services. If our solution is a luxury car, we'll have to provide our customers a driving experience. If our Customer Segment is wealthy business owners, a meeting with a financial tax advisor would be a part of the solution.

A business may have different sales approaches for different products, as well. For example, spare bicycle parts could be sold at an online store, but customers may like to try the helmet and glasses before they purchase them.

We should add the *Sales Approach* and dedicated resources to the **Table 1-4**. An example of an IT company. Please observe **Table 1-5** below.

TABLE 1-5

An example table of the *Go-to-Market Strategy* based on *Customer Segments Solutions* for an IT company.

	Customer Segments	Customer Segment Solution	Products	Sort of Deal	Customer Name	Resource	Sales Approach
1	CRM sales to large corporates	CRM sales with local support	CRM	Sales or Partnership	Alpha, Beta, Gamma	Account manager, CRM GM, Software team	On site meetings, Product adjustment
2	Stock management service	Stock management service	Stock	Service contract	Alpha, Delta, Epsilon	Salesperson, Stock expert	Calls, Online demo, Prove of concept
3	Small company package	Software for logistics package	AI , Stock, Accounting	Sale, Rental & Service	Theta, Iota, Kappa	Distributor	Calls, Online advertising, Create a bundle
4	Storage and Data management	Rental storage and database Management - end to end.	Storage + Database Management	Sale & Rental	Alpha, Beta, Gamma, Delta, Epsilon, Theta, Iota	Distributor Security expert	Response to tenders

Great! We've just created a *Go-to-Market* model!

Next, we must check the validity of our solutions with all the stakeholders involved in this solution. This includes salespeople, distribution, operation, R&D, finance, and customers. Connection to the customer is the most important aspect of this. Always get feedback from customers! Without this feedback, we are building a castle on sand.

STEP 5 - Look at the Big Picture and Avoid Big Mistakes in Planning

We've done the necessary research to build the right strategy for the new market. We found *Jobs-to-be-Done* and our competitive advantages. We also defined the needed resources for each market segment. Since we are extremely focused on customer needs, we may neglect the wider picture. There are three major cognitive biases we should consider before we move forward. These mental traps are well described in the book *Thinking Fast and Slow* by Daniel Kahneman. [8]

1. Avoid Winner's Curse, Always Check the Graveyard

Business research is mostly based on statistical analysis. The core of this research is the *Central Limit Theorem*. This theorem states that the sampling distribution of the sample means (mathematical average) approaches a normal distribution as the sample size gets larger — no matter what the shape of the population distribution. This holds especially true for sample sizes over 30.

This means that if we take more than 30 measurements, the averages of those measurements will have a bell shape (Gaussian distribution).

Let us look at an example based on the graphs below.

FIGURE 1-2

Dice Sum Central Limit Theorem, Wikipedia, by Cmglee. [9]

In the graph below, the horizontal axis, k, represents the average of n the experiments. The vertical axis (k), represents the probability(chance) to obtain the average k. So, if we roll a dice just one time (n=1) we will get unified distribution (same chance to get any face of a dice). But if we make an average of five rolls (n=5) the distribution will take a bell shape. The graph in the bottom right shows how distribution will have a smaller standard deviation as the number of experiments increases. By increasing the number of experiments, we increase the certainty about the average result of the tests.

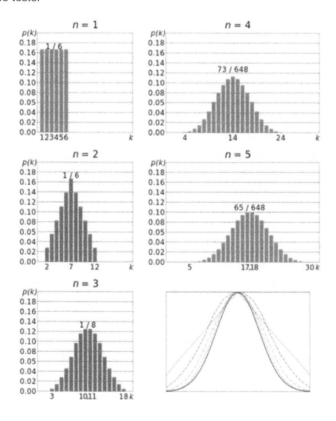

This is powerful and commonly used tool in the modern world. Using the *Central Limit Theorem*, we can find casualty in very sophisticated processes. This is vastly used in risk assessment, quality control, failure analysis, market research, medical research and more.

However, this great theory doesn't protect us from one of the biggest mistakes in statistical analysis. It is *sampling only the winners* and neglecting the losers. In other words, neglecting the graveyard of failed businesses.

There are numerous success gurus who summarize the attributes of winners and winning organizations in their books. The conclusions and ideas in these books are important and have helped thousands of people achieve their goals in life. The problem is that many of these books established their foundations on the study of winners and don't take samples that include losses, as well. This approach has a positive effect on motivating people, but it is dangerous for processes and strategies.

For example, let us assume we want to find a common denominator for leadership skills. We take a sample of 600 men who are well-known leaders. Then we examine 20 different personal qualities and build a statistical hypothesis connecting it with leadership skills. Next, we find statistical evidence that male leaders possess a distinguishing quality, say a wrinkle between their eyebrows. The population is large enough, the results are certain and there is a chance of only 5% that the hypothesis is false. Therefore, we could conclude that wrinkles between eyebrows may be needed quality for VP sales candidates.

With similar logic, we may conclude that to be an outstanding teacher in Israeli high school, you must give birth to a baby. The top 1% of Israeli teachers in high schools have given birth at least ones. The main problem in these studies is the scope of the research. Yes, the sample is big enough, but only the winners are indicated in the sample.

In the first example, most of the leaders had a wrinkle between their eyebrows. But what about the non-leaders? Do any non-leaders have a wrinkle between their eyebrows, as well? A wrinkle between eyebrows is not a leader's quality. Rather, it is common for men after the age of 40. A similar mistake was made in the best teacher survey. Both the top 1% and the rest of the 99% are mostly women over the age of 30. Teachers in the Israeli government educational system are mostly women. Most of them have given birth to a baby.

Every time we find a common attribute for the winners we must also check if it is common for the losers. We must observe both, not just pick the winners. You are probably thinking you wouldn't make this trivial mistake. Please think again...

In many organizations, managers seek the best script for a sales cold call only by examining the most successful calls. The best door-to-door salesmen are surveyed to find common qualities for the same reason. Product marketing strategies build long lists of best features but don't run a list of the worst features for a new product.

Most business self-help books establish their claims on the ground of the most successful companies. Even the best books sin in this domain.

Think and Grow Rich is the bible of personal achievement written by Napoleon Hill. [10] I think the ideas in this book are true, timeless, and extremely important. Napoleon conducted hundreds of interviews with the most influential people of his time.

However, Napoleon was focused only on the winners.

Another amazing book is *Good to Great* by Jim Collins. Collins researched 1,400 companies on the Fortune 500 since 1965. [11] Then he focused on 11 companies that sustained excellence over time. Yes, he examined the 1400 companies, but according to Collins, only 11 of them were the big winners. Some will claim that in the sample of 1400 companies there are both winners and losers. However, I could claim he examined 1400 winners. If a company made its way into the Fortune 500 list, it qualifies the company as a great winner, at least by my standards.

In summary, we need to take into account both the positive and the negative. If our solution solves one problem but customers hate the other features, it won't fly in the market. We must understand our disadvantages and avoid direct competition in those applications.

2. The Strategy should Match Our Company

"God grant me the serenity to accept the things I cannot change, the courage to change the things I can, and the wisdom to know the difference."
-Karl Paul Reinhold Niebuhr [12]

A friend of mine took the role of a country sales manager at an international semiconductor company. Part of his responsibilities was to plan and execute a *Go-to-Market Strategy*. He was well familiar with the Israeli electronic R&D market and had multiple connections with key decisionmakers. Since he had limited experience in sales management, As his friend, I aided him to understand the competition, Israeli market trends and relationships with partners. It took him six months to understand the dynamics of the Israeli market. Eventually, he resolved his ideas and presented them to the management. The leadership team embraced those ideas and agreed to carry them out. In the beginning, his Israeli partners were not convinced and resisted change. With strong pressure from the top managers, local partners agreed to give the new strategy a chance. After that, it took him some time to rebuild relationships with his partners.

My friend had a strong background in product management. With those skills, he easily identified major customers with needs aligning with the roadmap of his company. Those would be the key accounts in the Israeli market. He and his salespeople would focus on key accounts. This was a major part of his *Go-To-Market Strategy*.

Within one quarter, his salespeople had successfully established relationships with decisionmakers at the key accounts. He'd established communication between customers and product managers of his company. Managers at key accounts were excited about the roadmap of his company. They were waiting to use the future products in their designs as soon as the products were released.

Yet, with all the considerations, there was something he did not contemplate. This was so important and so fundamental that it shadowed all his successes. In the first year, he missed his sales target.

Every organization has its own culture, work ethic and mentality. It has its own risk virtue and willingness to invest. Even if the CEO of a company is fully committed, the middle-level managers must prioritize and invest resources. My friend made two assumptions which in retrospect proved wrong:

I. Middle-level management would be willing to deploy more resources to support the key accounts.

II. Execution of the roadmap and introduction of new products would happen as planned.

The middle-level managers decided not to deploy more resources to support the key accounts. Because of market trends, product line managers changed the roadmap and canceled many future products. As a result, my friend developed positive relationships with key accounts but did not have the products to sell them. Also, he didn't have people to support key accounts, so he couldn't generate enough revenue from those accounts.

From this experience, my friend learned an important lesson: *A good sales manager should know markets and products. A great sales manager should also understand his own organization, both its culture and its limitations.*

3. Preserve Alignment of Interests

A friend of mine had three children, all of them boys. His wife desperately wanted a baby girl. She really hoped their fourth child would be a girl. In Israel, in those days, the state-sponsored a pre-implantation Genetic Diagnosis (PGD) only for parents with four children with the same gender and with emotional distress. The thought was perhaps if you had four little boys at home, you would develop emotional distress. My friend had three boys. In a desperate attempt to change their fate, his wife found out about a special clinic run by an expert in his field. This doctor had developed a special technique to influence the gender of the baby by scheduling the sexual acts of the couple. This expert's business plan was simple. A couple would receive a detailed weekly schedule for their intimacy. In return, the expert would receive 5,000 shekels from the couple. If the treatment worked, the expert would keep the money. But if the expert could not help the right sperm cell win the race, the couple would get half of their money back as compensation. We do not need to be a game theory specialist to see that our expert's earnings had a mean value of 3,750 shekels.

Although the treatment was demanding, my friend and his wife were fully committed to the schedule. They slept less and skipped a few business meetings. As a result, their work ethic was harmed, but their relationship got much better. If you're wondering about the gender of the fourth baby...let's just say they got their 2,500 shekels back.

This arrangement didn't drive the doctor to put in extra effort. The doctor wasn't motivated to apply any effort because there was no large compensation for success. In addition, the extra effort wouldn't affect the final results, which were random.

The conclusion from this story is that the implementation of the strategy must drive the engagement and effort of the stakeholders. To find engagement, we should keep in mind two principles:

I.   The effort of the stakeholders should have a real impact on the results.
II. Reaching the target must lead to a large compensation for the stakeholders.

In summary, we should consider the motives of corporate colleges and local distribution partners. Successful people, in general, pursue their own interests over others. It is important to consider their willingness to apply effort. We should consider the profit of our channel partners. The ambition of our managers should be part of our plan, as well.

For more information, I encourage you to read about the Agency Problem. [13]

STEP 6 - Strategy Deployment

"When it comes to inferior generals and the way they use arms. They hear a lot but confuse themselves. They know a lot but doubt themselves. They are fearful of camp and hesitant in action. Therefore, they are likely to be captured by others."

We must do that, or we will fail.

People like to stick to the old ways and reject new approaches. They will neglect your research and try to implement known processes to the new market since those worked in the past. Your colleges and distribution partners may criticize your strategy and even you personally. You are the new guy and they've worked here forever. They may say you don't know what you're doing, and you should go home.

They may talk to your managers and influence them, as well. You should listen to their ideas but stick to your plans!

As we collect information and plan our strategy, we must consider multiple opinions and ideas. We have to be openminded and doubt every aspect of our strategy. This is necessary to obtain the facts from the market and accept reality. During the investigation phase, we should accept that we don't know everything.

As the strategy is defined and we are move into the execution phase, all doubts must be put aside. There will be a time to review the outcome of our strategy, but we must not do it during the execution phase. This strict implementation is a must to change existing processes and refocus our resources. We must execute our strategy and ignore the opposition.

Imagine top-down and bottom-up approaches. [14] [15] As we defined in the strategy investigation phase, the approach is bottom-up. The flow of information is upstream. We are collecting information from customers, partners, and colleges. We are in discovery mode. As we execute the strategy in the execution phase, the approach becomes top-down. The decisions flow downstream. We must change our organization and our market perception.

Usually, people oppose change. They will push back and disapprove. Your partner or colleagues may say they know their work better than you. They will suggest you don't know your job and will raise their concerns with your managers. They may put your plan to the test before you even have the chance to execute it.

This is a test of your character. You must be resistant to criticism and follow your vision. You have to believe in your strategy.

Market conditions are constantly changing, and all market participants are running simultaneously. Putting it in words of Carl von Clausewitz, "War is the realm of uncertainty."[16] There is no ultimate truth and no ultimate strategy. Many things during implementation will not go as planned.

The uncertainty, criticism and management pressure may get to you and add doubt to your work. You may start question yourself. This is dangerous ground upon which to walk.

If this happened to you, ask yourself the following questions:

- Are the research results still valid for today?
- Did you correctly choose the *Jobs to be Done?*
- Does customer choice make sense?

If we answer yes to all the above questions, then we must push forward with the execution. If not, it doesn't mean we have to drop the strategy. We can review and adjust but keep executing the strategy.

During the interview before a boxing fight, Mike Tyson's opponents described their strategy against Tyson. It was based on Tyson's height disadvantage. Tyson was shorter than his opponents and had a shorter arm reach. Tyson compensated for this disadvantage with unmatched striking power and the best defense at heavyweight deviation. The best strategy against Tyson was to keep the distance with straight punches and hug him whenever he got too close. Tyson's opponents were certain they could keep the pressure on and execute their plans during the fight. However, only the toughest opponents could stick to the plan, while the rest forgot it after a few blows form Tyson. When Tyson was asked about one of his opponent's plans, he said, "Everyone has a plan 'til they get punched in the mouth." [17]

So, in boxing terms, *we must have a big heart, a strong jaw and stick to the plan.*

Chapter Summary

"When the best generals use arms, they have the way of heaven above, the advantages of earth below and the hearts of men in between. Then they used them at the optimum moment, deploying them along with the momentum of the situation. This is why they have no broken troops or defeated armies. As for the mediocre generals, they do not know the way of heaven above and do not know the advantages of earth. They only use people and momentum.

Although they cannot be completely successful, their victories will be in the majority. When it comes to inferior generals and the way they use arms. They hear a lot but confuse themselves. They know a lot but doubt themselves. They are fearful of camp and hesitant in action. Therefore, they are likely to be captured by others."

The Book of Leadership and Strategy - Lesson of the Chinese Masters.

Imagine you are studying the earth below (products) and looking at the heaven above (customers). You plan and measure, consult and learn. You understand both the markets and the products. You efficiently deploy resources at the right time and in the right place. You motivate your people and lead them to victory. You don't doubt your plan, only adjust it if needed. You are certain, openminded and calm. You're going to execute and win!

Figure 1-3 provides a good visual flow chart to summarize this chapter.

FIGURE 1-3

Sellosophy flow chart for developing a *Go-to-Market Strategy* for new markets:

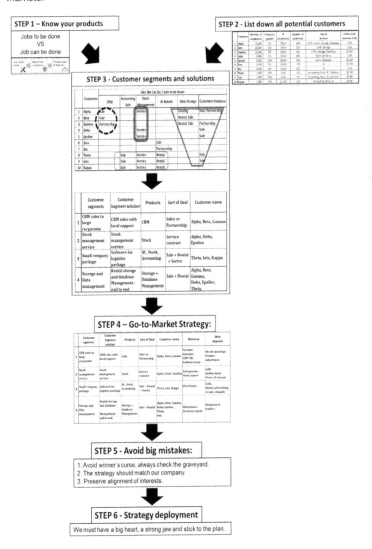

Chapter 2

Recruiting sales managers and business partners

In 1927, a young biologist in Ukraine, Soviet Union, made his first public announcement in the *Pravda* newspaper. He'd had success raising crops during cold Russian winters. It was a breakthrough in biology and agriculture for the Soviet Union. The new seeds were capable of withstanding the cold weather so farmers could raise crops three times per year. He called this method vernalization. This discovery turned the fields of Caucasus and Kazakhstan green during the winter, so the cattle didn't perish from poor feeding and the people weren't trembling about tomorrow. This remarkable achievement empowered him to transform Soviet Union agriculture and to influence other countries, as well.

This young scientist did most of the work by himself under the supervision of Nikolai Ivanovich Vavilov, the director of the *Lenin All-Union Academy of Agricultural Sciences*. Professor Vavilov supported him but with time became jealous of his success. Later, Vavilov strongly criticized his new genetic theory *Lysenkoism*. Only the government's involvement settled the dispute against Vavilov. *Lysenkoism* was accepted by the ruling party in the Soviet Union and by Josef Stalin in particular. Stalin ordered farmers to carry out *Lysenkoism* methods all over the Soviet Union.

Stalin also made this scientist the chief consultant on topics of plants and crops. His new ideas on the genetics of wheat were enforced on farmers all over the Soviet Union. In the 1930-40s, he had the most influence on farming in the world. Other countries such as China [20] followed the Soviet Union and carried out *Lysenkoism* as their leading method. The name of this outstanding young scientist was Trofim Lysenko.

The communist government in the Soviet Union and China forced thousands of farmers to execute Lysenko's methods, *Lysenkoism*. [18][19] This caused the death of over 37 million people from famine. Trofim Lysenko did not want to kill 37 million people. He wanted the recognition and the position of Director of Genetics at the Academy of Sciences.

We may assume that Stalin embraced Lysenko's idea because it resonated with communist ideology, not just to kill seven million people. We may also assume that the Chinese government ordering farmers to increase the density of planting did not aim to kill 30 million people. Both governments just made a terrible choice in hiring managers.

Trofim Lysenko was intelligent and a great speaker. He rose from poverty to become a scientist, a leader and eventually the director of the Institute of Genetics. He had all the shiny medals, the best recommendations, and the right resume. Trofim had also many critics, but they all became enemies of communism. Their voices were not heard.

I encourage you to read about Trofim, his rise to power and his pseudo-science. I illustrated the story above from Lysenko's point of view just to make a point. I see the *Lysenkoism* story as an example of the hazards of pseudo-science. It is a crime against humanity.

Some would say it could happen only in the Soviet Union and in the early days of communist China and not in a free country. Farmers in the Soviet Union could not criticize the government and had to follow orders. In a democracy, pseudo-science such as *Lysenkoism* could not possibly flourish. Pluralism and freedom of speech is our defense against this evil.

This is correct in principle. In his article *Science as Falsification*,[21] Karl Popper provided us with the definition of real science versus pseudoscience. According to Popper, a real scientific theory becomes stronger with criticism. Every genuine test of a theory is an attempt to falsify it. Every time that scientific theory passes a falsification test it becomes a better theory. Pseudo-science cannot stand falsification attempts.

Therefore, healthy criticism is beneficial for organizations. Successful strategies will successfully pass falsification tests and unsuccessful strategies will be abandoned. Good people will be promoted to leading positions. Charlatans and corrupted officials will be dismissed. In an organization with healthy criticism, the most successful people will be the true achievers. The least successful people will be pseudo-scientists. Therefore, the more successful the person is, the better he is at his job.

Following this logic, recruiting sales managers ought to be easy. In a democratic country, we should scout for the most successful candidates. The most successful should be the best.

There is one problem with this theory. I think in many companies there is no healthy criticism. Many organizations are not pluralistic.

Even in democratic countries, companies are not democratic. We have many examples of a lack of healthy criticism in large and small organizations. In startup companies, funders may be too in love with their ideas and neglect the business case. Large bonuses sometimes drive corporate executives to prioritize short-term over long-term profits. Government organizations have complex processes, so personal connections are sometimes more effective than talent and facts.

Thus, we will meet sales managers who could trick their way to success. Sales managers may have big smiles, strong handshakes, and impressive resumes. They will have expensive cars, imposing websites, and many success stories, yet some of them may be pseudo-scientists without any true achievements. Some sales managers with great resumes may be deadly to our organizations.

How should we select the right sales manager?

Let's start with something we can control. Let's start with our own attention and emotions.

Critical Thinking and Dealing with Emotions

"Take delight in mindfulness, guard your mind well."
-The Buddha [22]

Both Professor Dan Ariely and Professor Kahneman presented in their books what irrational decisionmakers we are. For a human, it is almost impossible to disconnect from his internal bios and grasp the moment as it is. Most of the time, we don't have the resources to think deeply about the problem. Instead, we use our intuition. If we pay attention and discipline ourselves, we can become rational, but this takes a lot of effort and focus.

In his book *Thinking, Fast and Slow,* [23] Professor Kahneman offers a model with two imaginary agents to represent intuition and analytic thinking. He called them *System 1* and *System 2*. *System 1* is automatic and impulsive. *System 1* manages most of our daily tasks. *System 1* is the autopilot of the mind. *System 2* is conscious and considerate. We turn on *System 2* to focus on a task. We use *System 2* when we are learning a new skill or solving a puzzle. Using *System 2* is difficult and running it for a long time is even harder. Recall, perhaps, the feeling you had after enduring a three-hour exam.

The table below provide good summary of this concept.

TABLE 2-1

A two-systems concept table based the book *Thinking, Fast and Slow* by Professor Kahneman. [24]

SYSTEM 1	SYSTEM 2
Fast and effortless	Slow and demand effort.
Automatic, we use it without focus	Demand focus and awareness
Jumps to conclusions regarding causality.	Makes up stories to either confirm or deny those conclusions.
Intuitive, impulsive and may be irrational.	Rational, finding solutions based on calculations

For further reading, please read the book *Thinking, Fast and Slow* by Professor Daniel Kahneman.

The problem is that we cannot fully suppress *System 1* and use just *System 2*. Every emotional distraction will get us out of focus and lead us to use irrational intuition (*System 1*). This is a human quality developed by millions of years of evolution. As our predecessors were running through the Eastern African Savanna, they had to think fast. They had no time for long consideration. Responses had to be automatic. If some big mammal attacked, we had a little time to calculate our retreat. The reaction had to be immediate. For our survival, *System 1* had to be in charge.

However, selecting the best candidate for a job requires a different skillset than running from predators. Interviewing requires a high level of focus, rational thinking, and analysis. This is a job for *System 2*.

Strong emotions may distract us and ignite *System 1*. It is a survival response designed by evolution, a necessity for our survival, yet a liability at business meetings, especially at meetings that require thinking. At interview meetings, there are many situations which may cause emotional thinking. For example, our thoughts may be on looking professional instead of focusing on candidate behavior. A good-looking consultant may evoke sympathy or lust. A tragic story may lead us to feel empathy or compassion. Some people will use those tactics without noticing, as it is part of their automatic subconscious behavior.

Professional negotiators use our strongest feelings to get us out of focus. Skilled salespeople use the feelings of fear and desire to close deals. For instance, during an interview, he will make you fear financial loss and desire promotion. Every time our mind wanders, we may think irrationally, using *System 1* when we need *System 2*.

We may find the solution to the described challenge in Buddhist philosophy. In some meditation techniques, we calm our inner voice and don't think about the past or future. Emotions may come and go, but we observe them from a distance. In this meditative state, we are not our emotions, neither are we our thoughts. Every time a skilled salesperson tries to evoke feelings of fear and desire, he will talk about the past or future. He will construct a picture in our minds of a positive future and connect it with his achievements. He will also frighten us with a negative future or remind us of our past failures. Let him do it. Don't fight it. Accept those images calmly. Smile at the images and refocus on NOW. You are not your emotions. You are the observer who accepts his own humanity.

Accept yourself as an emotional being, observe and acknowledge your emotions and then refocus on NOW and your present task.

> *"Let not a person revive the past*
> *Or on the future build his hopes;*
> *For the past has been left behind*
>
> *And the future has not been reached.*
> *Instead with insight let him see*
> *Each presently arisen state;*
>
> *Let him know that and be sure of it,*
> *Invincibly, Unshakeably.*
> *Today the effort must be made."*

The Buddha Gautama (Bhaddekaratta Sutta, MN 131) [25]

Deepak Chopra in his book, *Buddha: A Story of Enlightenment*, provides us with an interesting story. In his early years as a prince in the palace, The Buddha unexpectedly met the demon king Mara. In Buddhism, Mara is an evil demon who uses a mental weakness of men to control them--weaknesses such as fear, greed, lust and anger, the strongest emotions.

The encounter happened during an hour of darkness at the palace.

Buddha did not fight Mara's provocations but took a different path to fight the demon. Buddha sat still on the ground. He understood that he could defeat the demon not by resisting him but by finding a place in his mind that was safe from Mara. Buddha was not fighting his weaknesses but accepting them and then refocusing his mind on a place inside his mind where Mara was not present. [26]

For me, this safe place is NOW. The present moment. In the present moment, there is no fear or greed, nor pain of past failures, neither hope of future gains. Just the task in front of us. This story is about meditation. Meditation is not only a way to relax in a dark, quiet room but is an important tool in the business world. The ability to be present, accepting the mental pressure and still be focused during a meeting is a must-have skill. This skill needs to be repetitively practiced and eventually mastered.

Most of us are calm as we are watching TV at home or as we are listening to chill-out music and drinking wine. We should practice calmness under emotional pressure in the meeting room.

As we become calm and focused using *System 2*, we can move to the second step.

Assessing Candidates for the Job

1. Evaluation Model vs Intuition

Psychologist Professor Daniel Kahneman, a Nobel Prize laureate, suggests not to trust our personal judgment of people. In his book, *Thinking, Fast and Slow*, Kahneman shares his experience in the Israeli Army [27]. He learned in his days as a psychological evaluator for the IDF how hard it is to judge people through intuition. The army's interview procedure was "almost useless for predicting the future success of the recruits." Twenty-year-old military interviewers interviewed the new recruits. Those interviews decided the recruit's assignment based on their general impressions and intuition. This assignment determined the recruit's fate for their next three years of service.

After running a detailed survey of the evaluation process, Kahneman found no correlation between the interview and the actual performance of the recruits. This was surprising, since the interviewers were 100% sure they could predict soldiers' future performance. As an officer responsible for the evaluation process, Kahneman had to restructure the IDF evaluation process. In the new evaluation process, he used the insights of psychologist Paul Meehl. Meehl argued that a simple mathematical model is much superior to intuitive judgments. [28] Distinctly coring each personal quality and then adding all scores would lead to more consistent results than intuition. It would also aid the interviewer to produce repetitive evaluations, less affected by his personal moods.

This basically means the evaluation process needs to be split into five to seven characteristics which are scored separately. Then a total score can be calculated based on the importance of each characteristic.

After implementing Meehl's approach to the IDF requirement process, Kahneman found a positive correlation between the assessments and future performers. The old intuitive process didn't generate statistically significant results, while the new process was adopted by the IDF.

How can we implement Nobel laureate findings to recruit better sales managers?

Before the interview, we should agree on five to seven most important characteristics and prioritize them. During the interview, we should do our best to score each characteristic separately. Only after the interview has ended should we calculate weighted arithmetic means for the candidate. In this way, we will be more objective and repetitive in our evaluations. This will also assist us to see the pros and cons of each candidate. It is a good way to compare and rank candidates in a methodical way.

Table 2-2 illustrates this point. Each position has different vital characteristics. This chart may be used in interviewing a business development manager for a new market. We will put different weights for each characteristic and then score them based on our impressions during the interview. At the end, we will calculate a weighted arithmetic mean for the final score.

TABLE 2-2

Example of a candidate evaluation table for a business development position

#	Characteristic	Wight	Score
1	Personal and professional Integrity.	20%	6
2	Experience as business developer in focused market.	20%	9
3	Technical understanding of customer applications.	15%	3
4	Developing new partnerships with strategic customers.	15%	9
5	Self driven leader with hunter mentality.	10%	5
6	Strong research and analyze skills.	10%	2
7	Charismatic and positive personality.	10%	5
	Final Score (weighted arithmetic mean)	100%	6

2. Avoid Cognitive Biases

Now we have a process with which to evaluate candidates. We also have a technique to keep our emotions calm and be focused on the interview. Using *System 2* and evaluating methodology should increase our chances for success.

Yet, like all humans, we are vulnerable to cognitive biases. A cognitive bias is basically misleading intuition, something that feels right to us because it is presented in a certain way. Since the answer appears clear to us, we may ignore facts and empirical data which does not support our intuition. In this book, I would like to focus on the four most relevant cognitive biases for this topic. For more information about those and other cognitive biases, please read the book *Heuristics and Biases: The Psychology of Intuitive Judgment*, by Daniel Kahneman and Thomas Gilovich.[29]

Cognitive biases may lead us to ignore facts and data, yet we can overcome them. As we identify potential cognitive biases, we should ignore our intuition and analyze available facts. The following cognitive biases are relevant to the recruitment processes.

A. The Halo Effect

This is the tendency to like or dislike everything about a person — including things you have not observed. Our first impression of the candidate will be based on his resume, a great smile, and his expensive suit. Former employers from S&P 500 companies may have praised him on the pages of the *Wall Street Journal*. We need to accept that this will affect our judgment. Look at the facts and use math and critical thinking. Even if this celebrated sales manager is overconfident, remember...

Confidence is no measure of accuracy!

B. Preferring Stories over Data

When given pure statistical data, we generally make accurate interpretations of the data. But when given statistical data and a story that explains things, we tend to go with the story rather than statistics. We favor stories with explanatory power over pure data. Our brains have a difficult time with statistics and mathematical models, so we may choose the easy way.

In interviews, candidates usually tell stories about their former experiences. A relevant and large enough data sample must support those stories, so it is essential to focus and investigate multiple events and data points before trusting the story.

Remember, stories supported by facts are much better than

facts supported by stories. Therefore, each characteristic that the candidate wants to convey in the interview should be supported by several facts.

We should remember the famous saying:

> *"In God We Trust. All Others Must Have Data."*
> *- Brian L. Joiner.* [30]

C. Luck and Regression to the Mean

Sales managers love to take credit for positive random events as a direct result of their actions. Taking credit for positive results is good for self-esteem, yet it is not necessarily an outcome of excellence. Luck may play a role here.

"It is a mathematically inevitable consequence of the fact that luck played a role in the outcome...Not a very satisfactory theory — we would all prefer a causal account — but that is all there is," (page 179 of *Thinking, Fast and Slow*). When we remove causal stories and consider statistics, we'll observe regularities, which is called the regression to the mean. *Regression to the mean* means positive results will be followed by negative results. A positive outlier on the chart may be followed by a negative one.

For example, two quarters after the new CEO took over the company, earnings per share improved dramatically. Newspapers concluded that the new CEO had turned the company around. This conclusion needs to be checked statistically over a longer period of time. This company may experience a few positive quarters because of market conditions, often followed by negative quarters. The new CEO just got lucky.

FIGURE 2-1

Regression to the mean of a stock price

In the graph below, you can observe two successful quarters following two unsuccessful quarters of the stock price. You can also see the point in time when the new CEO took the lead of the company. Some would say it was his work that lead to the two successful quarters. A wider look on the graph leads us to another conclusion. The stock price is following historical trend. Sometimes it exceeds the trend and sometimes it follows behind. At average it is following the trend. This illustrates the principle of regression to the means.

A single success does not determine the quality of the candidate. We must study his past and examine his long-term track record of achievements. A positive trend over several quarters is an indicator of good performance, while one positive quarter is not enough. It may just be luck.

Ignore luck and examine the long-term trends.

D. Expertise vs. Experience

Electronic antennas engineers develop expertise over a decade. While talking with such experts, you will have the impression that they can see radio waves propagating through the air. This kind of intuition is difficult to develop in comparison to other fields of electronics. Wave propagation carries a large amount of uncertainty. Although the simulation software such as ANSYS and HFSS provides a good prediction of the actual results, physical testing is necessary. Why does it take a decade to become an expert in antenna design? The level of uncertainty is high, and the frequency of feedback is low. It takes time to learn the causes and effects of the design process.

On the other hand, when there is a direct connection between the action and the reaction, it is relatively easy to learn the outcome. It is easy to become an expert. When there are multiple parameters that cannot be measured directly, we call it uncertainty.

A real expert has developed his skill and professional intuition from thousands of tests with feedback. It takes time to develop skill, just as it takes time to collect that feedback.

Instant feedback is best for learning new skills. Talented people can also learn from the feedback provided during a reasonable time after the experiment. Let us take a simple example of learning to ride a bicycle. The feedback is immediate. Adjusting the center of mass helps to be stable.

Speed is your friend. If you stop, you will fall.

But what would happen if you got all your feedback from the ride after an hour? Suddenly, while eating dinner, you are pushed right, then left and then are thrown to the ground six times. Would you be able to connect your feedback to your actions? Tough, isn't it? Yet, with discipline and hard work, it can be done.

The key is to find a direct causality between action and feedback. The antenna engineer cannot observe electromagnetic waves and his feedback is not instant. Sometimes he needs to wait several weeks or months to test his design. Only then he can learn based on the feedback of lab and field tests. There are multiple parameters influencing the results. It is quite challenging to understand what went wrong with the design. Yet, with time, he'll start to understand the causality between his actions and the results.

Causality can be illustrated by a feedback loop. Engineers are familiar with the concept of Closed-Loop Systems. These systems achieve the desired condition by comparing the intention with the actual results. Then the feedback loop adjusts the next action to get closer to the desired result. With each cycle, it becomes closer to perfection. As you can see in **Figure 2-2**, it does this by having a separate feedback path. This path is constantly providing corrective feedback to the system. This is causality. The closed-loop concept provides a good demonstration of the causality principle.

FIGURE 2-2

Block diagram of a Closed-Loop System illustrating causality in a learning process.

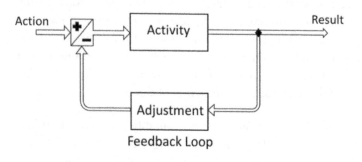

We may find experts in the fields of accounting, physics, martial arts, and agriculture. With talent and hard work, we can master all those professions. A surgeon, market researcher, program architect, team manager, sales professional and many more professions contain causality mechanisms and can be mastered.

On the other hand, I think in some professions the level of causality is so low that it is almost impossible to become an expert. For example, in political forecasting it is difficult to establish causality since feedback is provided after the starting condition has been changed.

Some psychologists have short-term feedback about a patient's mental health, yet they have a hard time following the patient after the treatment, so it is difficult for them to understand the effect of the treatment on the patient's long-term mental health. Nowadays, psychological sciences are conducting surveys and statistical analyses to find statistical causality in their treatments.

Sales managers must become experts in many technical and soft skills. Some skills may be developed by learning, but the best salespeople get their professional edge by practicing in the real world.

It is important to distinguish between experience and expertise. A distribution channel manager may have experience in direct sales, yet he is not a match to a key account manager. A key account manager has led many deals and has received direct feedback from past wins and losses. He's developed professional intuition and expertise in making complex deals with large organizations.

On the other hand, an account manager has limited advantages over a business development manager in matters of finding new markets. Business developers have accumulated expertise by trial and error over time. They also have some professional intuition about introducing new products, resource allocation and strategic partnerships.

In summary, people learning from feedback and causality can build expertise. Without feedback and causality, people cannot build expertise. They can only build confidence. Confidence without expertise is a recipe for disaster.

In the interview, it is important to understand how the candidate got his or her expertise. Was he able to get feedback at his former jobs? We need to understand how he established causality between his actions and results. Without it, we should not consider him as an expert.

Chapter Summary

The state of mind and techniques described in this chapter will aid in recruiting salespeople and business partners. Those techniques are useful in the choice of business partners, distributors, and business consultants.

The following flowchart will help you remember the workflow introduced in this chapter.

FIGURE 2-3

Chapter 2 Flowchart – Recruiting sales managers and business partners.

Salespeople can influence our emotions

Salespeople will present their best at meetings.
Salespeople will evoke emotions of greed, fear, trust & joy.
Salespeople will tell you interesting success stories.

Emotions can lead to irrationality (System 1)

Rational thinking (System 2) required mental effort and concentration.
Strong emotion leads to impulsive and reactive decision making.
Greed, fear, trust & joy, suppress system 2 and evoke system 1.

Focus on NOW

We shall reduce impulsive, irrational thinking (system 1) by focusing on NOW.
Accept yourself as an emotional being, observe and acknowledge emotions.
Refocus on the present time and the present task.   **Use System 2**

Evaluation model / table

Prepare a list of 5-7 ranked characteristics and evaluate them separately.
Use the model/table to compare between candidates.

Avoid Cognitive biases

❏ Hallo effect - Go behind the first impression.
❏ Preferring stories over data - Start with data first.
❏ Luck & regression to the mean - Examine the trend, ignore a lucky event.
❏ Experience vs expertise – No causality, no experts.

Chapter 3

Motivation of salespeople and business partners

"SPIRITUAL GOVERNMENT is the very best.
Next best is to make it impossible for people to do wrong. Next
after that is to reward the worthy
and punish the disruptive."
The Book of Leadership and Strategy –
Lessons of the Chinese Masters. [31]

Multiple books have been written on human motivation in the workplace. In this chapter, I would like to provide a summary and my point of view on motivating people in the workplace and adding structure. We will start from the strongest human motivational factors. At the end of this chapter, we will discuss tactics and games to motivate salespeople and business partners.

Motivation by Belief

"Spiritual government is the very best."

Historian and philosopher Professor Yuval Noah Harari claims that the biggest advantage of Homo sapiens over other animals is the ability to imagine not-existing things. [32] According to Professor Harari, Homo sapiens have the unique capability to imagine a narrative. Based on the imaginary narrative, humans can agree on a set of rules and believe in an imaginary hierarchical order. The earliest proof of this human ability was found in a German cave in 1939. In **Figure 3-1** we can see a picture of the Lion-man of the Hohlenstein-Stadel, a 35,000-year-old statue.

FIGURE 3-1

Picture of *Hohlenstein-Stadel*

The large 'Lion-man' statuette (Löwenmensch) was discovered in the Hohlenstein-Stadel, a German cave in 1939. [33]

It is a statue of a man with the head of a lion, a creature which does not exist in nature. Historians do not know if it was a statue of a god or some magical creature. Most researchers agree that people 35,000 years ago could build an imaginary story and articulate it to others.

Only humans can build a complex set of rules manifested in imagination. These imaginary rules are the basis of human culture, social hierarchy, religion, government, and financial structures. According to what we know today, our closest relatives, chimpanzees, cannot create imaginary beliefs about life after death. Even if one chimpanzee could think about it, he could not convince thousands of others to follow him. Scientists have found no community of chimpanzees that worships a god. There are no chimpanzees that will give away a banana now to get two bananas in the next life. [34] On the other hand, hundreds of millions of humans may believe in the same imaginary rules or stories. Humans kill for beliefs, neglecting the suffering they are causing to their kind and themselves.

In every culture, people believe in spirits, magic beings, and gods. Children are not born with those beliefs. Neither have they experienced those mythological creatures with their senses. Children are taught by others to have those beliefs.

Stepping out of the topic of religion, we can find even more examples. Looking into the business world today, all of us believe in the US dollar. We believe a dollar will have value and we will be able to use it. Bitcoin and Litecoin are bustling and booming as societies and governments approve and disapprove (believe and disbelieve) its validity. The main concern of the holder of a Bitcoin is if he can use it to purchase stuff. "Will the sellers of goods believe in the value of the Bitcoin?"

Both the dollar and Bitcoin are products of fictional stories which people have accepted. We cannot eat or drink a dollar, but we all agree on its value.

Not all imaginary rules are universal. Some are limited to small societies of a hundred people. Both religious sects and great startups have a strong belief that their work will change the world. Although the outcome of those endeavors is totally different, the human belief mechanism it is indeed similar.

Consequently, every organization must have a story in which they truly believe. In the business world, we call this a vision statement. For instance, the vision of Tesla is, "Tesla's mission is to accelerate the world's transition to sustainable energy."[35] Steve Jobs' vision statement for Apple in 1980 was, "To make a contribution to the world by making tools for the mind that advance humankind."[36] In 2020, NASA's vision was, "To discover and expand knowledge for the benefit of humanity." [37]

Some would think that a small organization does not need a vision statement. As a society including less than 50 people, it may operate without an imaginary story. The same as a group of 50 chimpanzees can cooperate together without imaginary beliefs. However, this would be only true if the organization in question was on an island in the Pacific Ocean and completely isolated from the external world. A startup is not the 10 employees listed on its financial statement. A startup is the employees, shareholders, banks, sub-contractors and most importantly, the customers. All the above must believe in the vision to make it happen—mostly the customers!

People will purchase our products only if they perceive that the value of the product is higher than the value of the money in their pockets. Therefore, our vision statement must reflect a higher value than all other alternatives. All our stakeholders must believe and tell our story to more people. If the story is trustworthy and beneficial, the value of our products will grow.

"WHEN A THOUSAND people are of like mind, they gain the power of a thousand people; when ten thousand people are of different minds, then no one is really useful. Only when commanders, soldiers, officials and citizens operate as one body can they do battle in response to an opponent.
-The Book of Leadership and Strategy –
Lessons of the Chinese Masters [38]

The first step in motivation is to articulate a vision statement. Then we must make all the stakeholders believe in the vision statement. As in the quote above, to be of *"...like mind, they gain the power of a thousand people."* Yet, it is not simple. Many organizations are failing in this domain.

Organizations are failing because their processes and rules are not aligned with their vision statements. Managers are not authentic. They are not living out their vision statements. To communicate the vision statement, companies use rituals such as seminars and company events. Companies also put slogans in their emails and on their websites. Rituals and slogans are important, but employees can see through the smoke. Smart people prefer actions over slogans. To make employees and customers believe, managers need to live their story. They need to be the vision statement, whatever the cost.

Religions such as Christians and Jews are well familiar with stories about martyrs who died for the sanctification of their God. By refusing to renounce their God, martyrs were sentenced to a painful death. By following beliefs, they paid the ultimate price. As a result, martyrs become symbols of religious values. They become stories for believers to tell.

Luckily, in the business world we don't need to die in agony to prove our loyalty to the company's vision. However, we should use similar techniques to make employees believe in our vision statement. Successful leaders authentically do this by paying the required price. They prefer their values over all other gains.

Yvon Chouinard, the founder of Patagonia, wrote a book called: *Let My People Go Surfing: The Education of a Reluctant Businessman*. In his book, he introduces his philosophy on business. Yvon not only talks the talk but walks the walk. Patagonia employees can leave the office for a perfect surf whenever they want. Yvon follows his beliefs whatever the cost it. He prioritizes surfing over immediate profits. [39]

Zappos is an online shoe and clothing retailer. Every new hire at Zappos must spend four weeks at a call center. It doesn't matter if the new hire is a programmer or a VP. They must all start by taking calls from customers as call center reps. This action demonstrates Zappos new employees that listening to customers is their way of life. [40]

Managers of Twitter believe employees should constantly learn. They want their employees to feel they've learned something new every week, so they created *Twitter University*. *Twitter University* trains company employees and assists Twitter to publish great content. This university is helping Twitter recruit young and ambitious talent. The company prioritizes university activities and key Twitter employees run the lectures. [41]

"People are the body of the commanders, and the commanders are the heart of the people. If the heart is true, the limbs and body follow it closely. If the heart is suspicious, the limbs and body are out of control. If the heart is not single-minded, the body does not regulate its strength. If commanders are not sincere in their need, soldiers are not brave and bold."
-The Book of Leadership and Strategy –
Lessons of the Chinese Masters [42]

Belief in a big cause is a vital part of human nature. It gives us a reason to wake up in the morning. It gives meaning to our lives.

The sincere belief in a vision statement gives employees a true reason to strive for success in their careers and a reason to be loyal to the company. A reason to spend less time with their families. A reason to overwork and be underpaid. A reason to deal with failure and stay when the future looks dark.

Write a vision statement, the story of your organization. This is your reason to be. Believe in your story and live your story! Slogans and rituals will not do. Only real action will make people follow your vision. If you believe, people will follow.

"If we possess our why of life,
we can put up with almost any how,"
-Friedrich Nietzsche, 1889. [43]

Motivation by Human Needs

"Next best is to make it impossible for people
to do wrong."

The initiator of humanistic psychology, Abraham Maslow, proposed a hierarchy of needs in his paper, *A Theory of Human Motivation.* [44] Maslow published his theory in 1943. Many sociologists and philosophers reused and developed his ideas in their works, yet the basic concept stays the same. We are motivated by our needs. To feel a need for a higher level, the lower level needs must first be partially satisfied. A classic representation of the hierarchy of needs, a pyramid with five levels, is illustrated in **Figure 3-2**.

FIGURE 3-2

Maslow's hierarchy of needs in form of a pyramid:

There is much to be said about each need, but it is out of the scope of this book. I encourage you to read more about Maslow's Hierarchy of Needs, starting with his paper, *A Theory of Human Motivation*, A. H. Maslow (1943). [44]

It is important to keep in mind that a need does not have to be fully fulfilled in order for a person to feel a hunger for a next-level need. A person may be looking for affection and belonging even at times of war when his safety is not guaranteed. A woman may have a strong ambition to prove herself even if she feels unloved by her parents. **Figure 3-3** illustrates this concept very well.

FIGURE 3-3

Dynamic hierarchy of needs of Abraham Maslow for the article of based on the article, *Dynamic Hierarchy of Needs of Abraham Maslow* referring to Krech, D./Crutchfield, R. S./Ballachey, E. L. (1962), Individual in society, Tokyo etc. 1962, S. 77 [45]

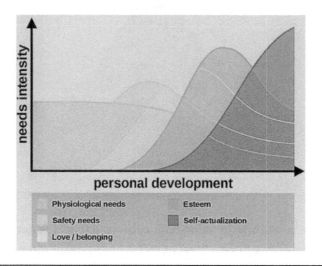

In this illustration, the needs overlap with each other. Even when a person proceeding higher need as esteem, his basic need for food is still important. Yet, this person is driven by his esteem need rather by his hunger. Maslow claimed that a lack of safety for a fed person will be as painful as a lack of food for a hungry person.

Lack of belonging is as painful as a lack of a feeling of self-accomplishment. According to Maslow, a sociologically healthy person will strive to fulfill all his needs, one after another. The higher a person is on the pyramid, the better he feels.

According to Maslow, the ultimate goal is to reach self-actualization, a feeling of self-fulfillment, the feeling that we are making a difference by doing what we love to do.

Maslow described self-actualization: *"A musician must make music, an artist must paint, a poet must write if he is to be ultimately at peace with himself. What a man can be, he must be. This need we may call self-actualization."* [46]

As illustrated in the graph, the higher the need, the more effort is required to satisfy it. Therefore, our employees will work harder to fulfill higher-level needs.

For example, after a 24-hour fast at Yom Kippur, I feel extremely thirsty and hungry. Yet, after just one burger and three glasses of water, my physiological needs are fulfilled. Another burger will not make me much happier. On another hand, in a search to fulfill my self-actualization needs, I invested months of my life in writing this book. Yet, I have a long way to go until I will feel truly self-actualized.

Looking at the challenge of motivating employees from this perspective, we may conclude that the higher needs will lead to a higher dedication at work. We will get much more from our employees if we will let them fulfill their higher needs at our company.

Generally speaking, we may assume that the chief technology officer (CTO) comes to the office not just to feed himself and his family. The CTO is willing to fulfill his higher needs at the workplace. He is seeking ways to bring new technology to the market and influence the entire industry. A janitor comes to the office to fulfill other needs, probably lower end needs such as physical needs and belonging needs. The janitor may have after-work activities where he fulfills his upper-level needs of esteem and actualization.

It is common to find the CTO staying after working hours and traveling abroad for business. Is it just to bring more food to the family table? I don't think so. The CTO is getting much more than just food from this arrangement. The CTO is enjoying himself and is fulfilling his higher needs such that he is willing to sacrifice his free time for it.

Maslow claimed that this striving to fulfill our needs is a part of human nature. So, we may ask, why are not all mature and healthy people totally fulfilled?

The answer is simple. We are living in an uncertain environment. There is healthy competition on physical and psychological resources. A certain man can truly love only one woman at a time. In a certain company, there is only one position of Art Director. At a boxing match, there will be only one winner. Therefore, there are hardships to overcome in order to fulfillment of a need.

As people invest their efforts to achieve a higher need, they may lose lower needs. This is a big risk, since lower needs are more fundamental. By fulfilling a need for self-esteem by rising upward on a company ladder, a person may lose his social circle of coworkers. A toddler boy will not investigate a new house by himself since he is afraid to leave his mother's protection. Two knights fighting for the love of a young lady may be injured in the sword fight.

Fear of losing what we already have may stop us from fulfilling our higher needs. Therefore, some people stay at positions that cannot fulfill their higher needs.

The paper *Prospect Theory: An Analysis of Decision under Risk* (1979) published by Daniel Kahneman and Amos Tversky[48] presents a good explanation for such behavior. This innovative idea granted them a Nobel Prize in economics. People hate to lose more than they are likely to gain. See the graphs in **Figure 3-4**. People will be more emotionally impacted by losing $1000 than gaining $1000. Financially, the gain and loss are the same. Yet the pain of a loss is much stronger than the joy of a win.

From an emotional standpoint, if we lose $10,000 on the stock market, we must gain more than $10,000 to overcome the pain of our loss. If we just gain $10,000, we will still feel an emotional burden.

Let's demonstrate this notion with the example of John. John got a job offer from a competitor firm and considering taking the job. The curved graph in **Figure 3-4** illustrates his personal preferences. The curve represents John's personal emotional impact of financial gain and loss.

In the *Graph* I, **Figure 3-4**, the salary and benefits in the new job are the same as in the current job, so John should feel good about taking the new job. Although John will not be financially impacted, he won't take the new job. The potential loss of the old job will impact John's emotions much more than the gains of the new job. John experiences the losses much stronger than the gains. To break even emotionally, John must gain more in salary and benefits on the new job.

The second graph in **FIGURE 3-4** illustrates another situation. John gains much more than he is losing by leaving his former employer. In this case, John is at an emotional equilibrium and may choose to pursue the new position.

As you can see, the new employer needs to overcompensate John for him to make the move.

FIGURE 3-4

Graphs illustrating the *Prospect Theory* on an example of John's preference to change jobs.

Graph I

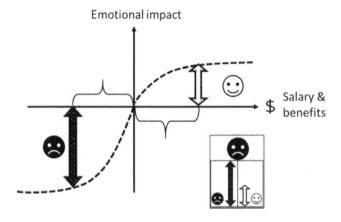

Graph II

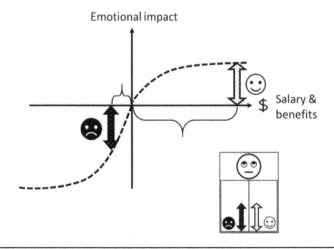

I think this is one of the main reasons people stay in their current situation rather than take risks. People accept their destiny and don't seek to fulfill their esteem and self-actualization needs. The risk of losing their lower-level needs is too high for them. Therefore, we see people neglecting their dreams.

In 2005, I joined the Israeli Defense Forces (IDF) to serve six years as a technical officer. I was involved in many R&D projects and learned a little about electronics and management. With those skills, I could easily find an occupation outside the IDF. In 2011, the Israeli high-tech industry was in excellent shape, so I could triple my income by demobilizing.

Our colonel saw this hazard to his unit. If all the good people demobilized, no one would stay to preserve the technical advantage of the IDF. The IDF could not compete with high-tech companies on financial benefits. Our colonel had to take another tactic. He emphasized the risks and hardships of the high-tech market. He spoke about booms and busts, about long hours and unemployment rates after the age of 45, and he did it in colors. After several conversations with our colonel, I had a dark picture of my future in the high-tech industry. I imagined myself working 14 hours a day, divorced, and separated from my children. Those fears prevented technical officers from leaving the IDF. Some of my peers traded their dreams for stability. In their minds, the benefits were not big enough to compensate for the potential losses.

Every person goes to work to fulfill several of Maslow's needs. Our job is to position each worker at the relevant level on the hierarchy of needs. We should provide him with the ability to fulfill his needs through work. Each position in our organization could fulfill several needs, but not all positions can fulfill all five needs. Therefore, not every storekeeper can reach a high level of self-actualization at his job. If this person starts to seek self-actualization through his work, he should be promoted. He may also leave the organization in search of a new, more fulfilling position. On the other hand, we should not hire a VP of Sales who just wants to survive (fulfill his basic needs). We should hire a VP of Sales who is seeking self-actualization through work achievements, a person who has a will to succeed so strong he feels actual pain in his gut.

FIGURE 3-5 demonstrates this notion by positioning the emotional benefit axis on the model of the graph of dynamic hierarchy of needs.

Each employee in our company may fulfill different needs at his position. As we assigned people to relevant positions, we should keep them engaged by reaching an equilibrium between their will and fear.

By cultivating too much anticipation for self-actualization, we may create feelings of unfulfillment which will eventually create tension and employees leaving. Too little anticipation of personal growth will cause an employee to display passive behavior. In the long run, this will kill our organization.

FIGURE 3-5

Graph of employees' personal preferences to risk positioned on the graph of dynamic hierarchy of needs.[49] This figure illustrates the development of employees and their preferences to seek personal development at work.

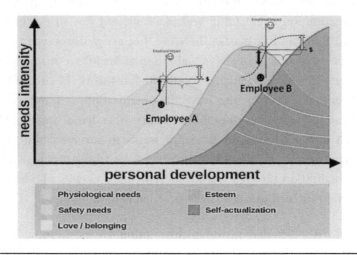

Please don't take me wrong. Fear is not necessarily bad for us and our people. A reasonable amount of fear of losing basic needs such as esteem and love will keep employees at their current positions. This fear may even make them happy. Every day, they choose to stay at their jobs, since the alternative is much worse. Employees will feel good since they made the right decision for themselves and their families.

We've all experienced gratitude for our lives and accusations after a dangerous event. We'll say, "It gave me perspective on what is important in life." This means, "I am thankful for the food on my table and my lovely family. I don't need more than that now." So, reminding employees about negative alternatives may motivate them from time to time.

Be aware of enduring too much fear. This is dangerous for the organization. In this case, people won't think about the future of the organization, but rather their self-preservation. Fear is contagious, like an epidemic. It destroys trust and kills initiative. It is a slippery slope for any organization. The balance between the will to gain and fear of loss is the sweet spot of motivation. This is the essence of personal motivation by human needs.

We should understand which needs our employees want to fulfill and how they prefer to do that. We also need to know what they are afraid to lose. By applying this knowledge, we can make a super-achiever out of an ordinary employee. We can help our people to grow and reach self-actualization at work.

Motivation by benefits

*"Next after that is to reword the worth
and punish the disruptive."*

There are times when an organization cannot implement the former strategies. Our people don't believe our story since company management doesn't live the story. Managers have a hard time understanding the individual needs of our employees and can't build an infrastructure to fulfill those needs. Managers don't see their work as a way to self-actualize. They look outside our organization to fill this hole in their lives. In this situation, people will see work as a necessity, something they must get done. They'll think twice before putting in extra effort.

This situation isn't hard to spot. The main symptoms are:

1. Management meetings without an actual outcome and execution.
2. The most productive and performance-driven people are leaving the company.
3. Employees complain about the company as an entity and not about individual managers.
4. In non-formal conversations, mid-rank managers don't understand company roadmaps and vision.

In these organizations, to motivate our people, we have no other choice but to create simple personal interest. This simple personal interest may be monetary or social.

A monetary personal interest can be a small bonus given to the sales manager who reaches his quarterly target. It may also be a prize, such as tickets to shows, vacations and presents. This should be something valuable to the employee that he can take home or use to his own personal benefit. Money is the most obvious compensation. Everyone wants to receive money. Yet, there may be more efficient ways to compensate employees.

Money is expensive compensation to the company. With time, people get used to a certain amount of financial benefit and expect them, so the company ends up paying more to obtain similar results. Also, most financial transactions from the company to employees are subjected to taxes. As a result, if the company is paying the employee $100, his family will get about $70 or less.

There are other ways that are more efficient benefits than money, ways that maximize the impact of our dollars on employee motivation. Gifts that will immediately benefit the employee are preferred over money. For example, we can buy him the best office chair in the market or upgrade his computer. We may approve the expenses of a home office, including furniture of the employee's choice. There are other options—sponsored vacations after a business trip, a car upgrade, laundry service or scholarships for him and his family members. Those alternatives are much more efficient than simple monetary bonuses. Those kinds of compensations create a strong link between the family of the employee and the company. If the family of the employee is happy, then the employee will have much more to lose if he leaves the company.

Therefore, we have to invest some time in learning about our employees' wants and needs. Sometimes we may be wrong, so it's be best if we just ask. We may also provide several options from which to choose. People bestow much more value to benefits they chose themselves than the ones somebody else chose on their behalf.

We may also use the *Prospect Theory* to our advantage. As we previously discussed, people are much more responsive to loss than to a win. Losing a certain amount of money will affect them much harder than winning the same amount. Perhaps we can give bonuses upfront and take them if the target was not achieved. In such a way, we increase the influence of the compensation and save money for the company. Yet, this approach puts a lot of stress on our people. In general, it should be our last resort.

An important aspect is to keep the actual numbers a secret. Coworkers should not know the size of the actual compensation. If we reveal it, they may start to compare it with their peers. This will backfire, as some employees will think they got less than others and will be disappointed.

We should tell our employees they received unique compensation and only 2% of the company received it this year. We should tell them their immeasurable personal contribution to the organization is in the top 5%. Since it is not measurable, it should be kept a secret and will not create envy among their peers. In this way, they will keep it to themselves.

This kind of motivation is not as good as believing in the company's vision, yet it will keep the wheel spinning.

Not all benefits involve money and presents. Humans enjoy emotional benefits, as well. People tend to feel good if they help a friend in need.

In his book *Predictably Irrational*, Dan Arielly described a social situation in which a person would be happy to help us for free but would not help us if we offered him money. This is part of our social norms. It is part of being social and friendly.[47]

For example, if we see that our neighbor needs help to change a tire while we are driving home from work, we may stop our car and help him change the tire. We would do it as an act of goodwill and feel good about ourselves since we helped another person. But what would happen if this person suggested paying us $10 for our work? Now our reaction may be totally different. In this case, we may insist on a fair deal. We should earn more than $10 per hour. Skipping a family dinner would cost us much more than $10. We may even be offended by the proposal. Now it is no longer about helping a fellow driver but being an employee. The monetary transaction won't give us a warm filling. There are multiple situations in life that have social rules and not business rules. Humans address them differently.

We can use social rules to motivate our people. To do that, we must disconnect the monetary compensation from an act of goodwill. Mixing them both will create the opposite effect. The following guidelines may be useful for social motivation:

1. Always provide a humane reason, if possible.

People will be more motivated if you provide them with a reason. A humane reason is even better. A salesman will be much more motivated if you explain to him that he is the hunter who brings food to the table of his tribe. Families of R&D, operation and production rely on his ability to close deals. If he closes the deal, all employees and their families will benefit. An R&D manager may be motivated by the notion that his technology will help people to connect. A marketing manager may be convinced that his messages will help our customers make better business choices.

2. Do it for your peers!

People will work harder if coworkers rely on them. A project manager may politely show the architect that quality control engineers urgently need to have his document to progress in their work. They rely on him.

3. Create healthy competition and praise winners.

We are wired to compete. Although some of us will not state that openly, we crave recognition. It raises our self-esteem and provides feelings of respect. The louder we praise our winners, the more it will motivate employees to win in the next competition.

Make the competition honest, specific, and BIG!

The most important aspect of competition is making it fair. If people doubt the fairness of the competition, it may backfire and create a strong opposite effect.

Both emotional and monetary benefits should be given as soon as possible. To have a maximal impact on behavior, we should reward the employee as he successfully completes his task. This will also demonstrate to his peers that good results lead to recognition, which will then drive people to work harder to reap the rewards. The more we wait with the reward, the less it'll be connected to the accomplishment. Perhaps, the lucky guy will remember why he got the prize, but his peers will not.

Chapter Summary

There are three levels of human motivation.

1. Motivation by Belief

   The most effective way to motivate is to make your employees truly believe in your vision.

2. Motivation by Fulfilling Human Needs

   If your organization is helping employees fulfill their human needs (Maslow), they will happily do their best at work.

3. Motivation by Benefits

   In some cases, it is difficult to use the above motivators. In those cases, you can provide employees with benefits. Benefits may be money and gifts, but it may also be emotional benefits.

FIGURE 3-6

Summary of Chapter 3, Motivation of Salespeople and Business Partners, in the form of a lever. This illustration will help us remember relevant ideas.

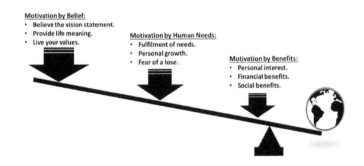

"Give me a lever and a place to stand and I will move the earth." - Archimedes of Syracuse. [50]

Chapter 4

Key Account Management: A broader view

Before getting into a discussion about account management, I would like to emphasize the cost of having account managers in our organizations. Account management is a long-term and demanding activity done by costly experts. Good account managers must have both technical expertise and a business orientation, a combination that is hard to find. Therefore, I think an organization should consider having account managers. As the decision of having account managers is made, accounts should be carefully chosen. These accounts should have the potential to bring enormous amounts of revenue into the company.

A direct account management approach should add value. If it is not adding value, we should instead rely on regional salespeople and distribution channels. In each account, we should define the level of engagement and the resources in which we plan to invest. For this task, we can use the methods described in Chapter Two of this book, *Business Development and getting into New Markets.*

> *"He will win who knows when to* fight
> *and when not to fight."*
> *-Sun Tzu, Art of War.* [51]

There is numerous literature available on key account management. There is a lot of material on how to map an account and build account plans which include tables, lists, charts, and forms. I find them useful, yet I have the feeling it misses the essence. The core of key account management is a deep understanding of our customers. It means knowing the intrinsic nature of organizational culture, processes, and available resources, both in the present and future. In the end, what guides me is not forms and templates but an understanding of the account.

The Key Account Manager (KAM) is the most complex level of a B2B (business-to-business) selling role without direct reporters. In general, KAM handles growing sales with the most important customer. Some may say KAM is just a salesperson focusing on several accounts. She is not. The KAM is more than a salesperson. She is an expert on specific tier-one accounts. The KAM contributes to our organization by having a unique knowledge of our most important customers.

What does the KAM have to do to be an expert?

To answer this question, let us consider the topic of her expertise. Let us think about a customer organization.

What is an Organization?

The dictionary definition of an organization is *a group of people who work together in an organized way for a shared purpose.* The organization could be a university, the government, an army, a private company, a charity, or a mix.

I suggest the following model based on the *Four Elements Model of a Successful Business Model* by Professor Clayton Magleby Christensen at Harvard Business School. [(52)]

Professor Christensen builds a model of an organization based on four elements:

1. **Customer Value Proposition**
   A way for company to supply customer demand and provide value to customers in products and services.

2. **Resources**
   Technology, people, products, machines, IP, data base, cash and more.

3. **Processes**
   Market research, product development, internal and external communication, customer engagement, booking orders and more.

4. **Profit Formula**
   The criteria used to prioritize activities. Gross margin, market share, ROI, customer satisfaction, funnel of opportunities, leads (MQL, SQL), sales targets and more.

I think that there should be a fifth element in this model.

5. Organizational Culture

Cambridge Dictionary defined organizational culture as *the types of attitudes and agreed ways of working shared by the employees of a company or organization.*

Culture is something that you notice when you spend enough time at the customer site. It is the meter of how they talk to each other and how they do business.

Great companies have a strong culture of sharing information, creativity, and innovation. People will be inspired by their work and may inspire us, as well. Yet, there are other cultures that might emerge. In the case of a shrinking company, people who stayed at the company may develop a survival culture. Members of academia may have a culture of competition based on prestige, leading to uncooperative behavior. Political activists engaging in a political movement may accept a leader's unethical behavior. Culture is not always at the whole company level. Different teams within a company may develop a special subculture. They will still share company values, yet their team dynamic will differ.

For example, in sales, we may find two sales teams that have totally different cultures. Although they are part of the same sales organization, one team may be hunters looking for big opportunities. The other team may have a farmer's culture. Farmers collect a lot of small, non-strategic orders from the market. Both teams may have a similar number of people and use the same company CRM, but their culture is different.

For me, culture is not a separate element of an organization that can be studied as a process. Culture is expressed in every aspect of management. Culture reveals itself at the execution of every process.

Figure 4-1 show the relationships between the elements of organization and the influence of culture on each element.

FIGURE 4-1

Relationships between the elements of an organization and the influence of culture.

As we define customer organization, we should discuss the tools account managers need to prepare to understand and manage business relationships.

Account Summary and Account Plan

To become an expert on a certain account, we have to understand the four elements of our customer's organization. We don't need to understand all divisions of the company, just the relevant divisions for our business. For example, account managers selling cloud storage will need to know the IT organization. Account managers selling electronic components must know the R&D organization.

There are multiple templates and softwares that can help organize information about accounts. Each company uses a different template, so I prefer not to cover it in this book.

I would like to make a list based on the four elements described above. Each element has several ingredients which we need to understand to see the full picture. Finding this information is the KAM's responsibility.

1. **Resources:**
   a. Organization charts
   b. Available assets
   c. Gaps and areas of limited resources
   d. The estimated budget for new projects
   e. The division's yearly budget
   f. The number of employees
   g. List of former years' purchases
   h. Organizational growth rate

2. **Processes:**
   a. Organization structure

    b.   Key decisionmakers

    c.   Decisionmaking processes

    d.   Purchasing processes

    e.   Budget allocation process

    f.   Business seasonality

3. Profit Formula:

    a.   Financial reports

         i.   Grows margin

        ii.   Revenue of each product line

      iii.   Relevant to our business spending (R&D, sales activities, loan payment and more)

    b.   Project schedules and targets

    c.   Organization Key Performance Indicators (KPI)

4. Culture:

To obtain a feeling of an organization's culture, we need to spend some time at the company and observe human interactions.

Culture is a wide concept, so there are no specific indicators. I suggest you can feel the culture rather than summarize it, yet there are several aspects which may help us better understand the culture.

    a.   The number of managerial layers

    b.   The mix of gender, nationalities, and age of the employees

    c.   Turnover

    d.   The sense of urgency and level of dedication

    e.   Level of risktaking

    f.   Integrity

This level of customer understanding is the first step in account management. It will help us to build account plans and justify the allocation of resources. Based on this information, we will plan our tactical moves to win customers over and promote our products. With this level of customer intimacy, we are not just a supplier but a partner, a member of the customer's team.

As a project manager can present his project progress and budget to management, the account manager must present the current status and forecasts. As a product manager articulates product features and advantages, we have to present the business situation and our product fit.

To present our findings to members of the sales team and management, we have to prepare an account summary. An account summary is a practical document that helps us to plan our activities and win major deals. A good account summary should be based on the following aspects:

1. Organization Charts and Relationship Charts

Organization charts and relationship charts are the fundamental tools for planning our activities inside the account. This is a visual map of an organization. On this map we should include managers, key decisionmakers, promoters and opponents. This map should be something between a company organizational chart and a detective pin wall like in movies. It is a visual presentation as a diagram of the relationships between potential customers, promoters and blockers. We may also add color coding and comments.

Figure 4-2 provide a basic example of a chart that can be used by an account manager selling software security products.

FIGURE 4-2

Example of an organization and relationship chart.

People who like our products are colored in gray. People who do not like our products are marked in black. As you can see, if Dave gets the promotion to the Software Director, it will help us. Also, we could change Tim's mind by working with his friend Rick. If we don't yet have a relationship with the CEO, we could invest in our relationship with Nike, the VP R&D. With the help of the CFO and VP R&D, we can lead the CEO to choose our solution.

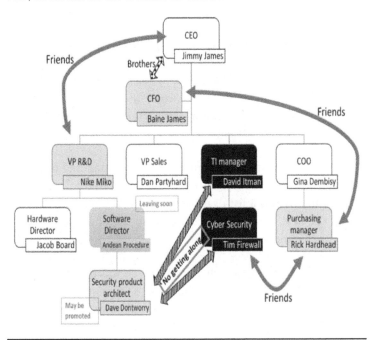

2. Account Economics and Purchasing History

This will help us to estimate the TAM (Total Addressable Market) for this customer, set targets and track our progress. Most of the data is on the web. It is best to meet with the purchasing department and company management to validate our findings.

3. Funnel of Opportunities

This is a list of opportunities (projects) on which we are working. It should contain the size, schedule and major milestones for each project.

4. Solutions Description or a Block Diagram

A funnel of opportunities is a list of projects we need to win. Each major opportunity needs to have a description of the solution. A solution description may be a block diagram with comments or a list of retirements.

Based on the account summary and understanding of our offering, we will be able to construct an account plan. An account plan is a list of prioritized activities we should do in the next 12 months. Each activity should have a time schedule and assigned person.

Yes, I agree things are changing fast and this plan may not be valid in three months. Yet, let's remember we are entering into a new account. It's an unknown territory for our company. We collected all this data to coordinate all the parties involved. We have to sit down and write the course of action for our team. We should present and inform all parties involved in this plan.

As the account unfolds, we will adjust and improve, but we need to have a starting point, which is an account plan.

> *"...plans are worthless but planning is everything."*
> *-President Dwight D. Eisenhower* [53]

Positioning

As account managers, we are the face of our company. We are a single point of contact for the customer with all parts of our organization.

The account manager's most important task is to position themselves in the right way. What does this mean?

Many salespeople would say we should become friends with key customers in the account. A deep personal relationship is a great asset for the account manager. Yet, I claim that friendship does not lead to sales. Friendships are helpful for opening doors and obtaining information, but if we want to get orders, we must have something more important.

Credibility.
Let's take an example from our lives. Assume you have a new opening at your company for a senior product planner. You have several friends who come from a product management background. As you wonder about the best fit, you'll probably focus on their work-related abilities. The fact that you got drunk with a certain friend two weeks ago is not as important as his expertise. You haven't worked with your friends, so you don't know how good they are at their jobs. You'll probably speculate about their professionalism based on their

interactions with you. Probably, for the product manager role, we will not choose the most friendly guy. Instead, we choose the one who can best do the job.

I think it is the same in our work as account managers. We may use friendships to get in, but if we want the deal, then credibility is the most important aspect.

Credibility is defined as *the power of inspiring belief.* Having credibility will make customers choose our solutions and services over the competition. Since credibility is so important, let's break it down.

There are three aspects of credibility with customers:

1. **Expert**

    The customer should know we are capable of solving problems in a professional way. Demonstrate a high level of technical and commercial knowledge.

2. **Powerful**

    Customers want to deal with the ones who call the shots. If there are any difficulties, he'll have the resources to solve them. Account managers must position themselves as powerful decisionmakers and their company as a powerful supplier.

3. **Character**

    People do business with people. We must convey trustworthy and positive personalities. The best way to do that is to be trustworthy and positive. Be open and honest, share information and aid customers. Care about the person who stands in front of you, not just about the deal. Align deeds with words.

Managing the Account — Short and Long-Term

Each big deal is different. In every situation, we have to apply common sense and progress in an unknown environment. One visual analogy helps me do my job.

Imagine a large and complex deal as a chess game. Instead of wooden figures, we have real people—people with personalities, abilities and preferences. As you position figures, you cannot control their actions. The only thing you can do is to position them in certain locations on the chessboard. We may ask our colleagues to act in a certain way, yet they have their own characters and abilities. Our influence on our customer figures is much lower than on our colleagues. We cannot even position them, much less influence their actions.

In this surrealistic chess game, as in a real one, we have different members on our team. We have application engineers, product line experts, product line managers, sales managers, salespeople, marketing and distributors. Customer figures may include system engineers, expert engineers, project managers, high-ranking managers, buyers and external advisors. There is a dense fog covering the chessboard, and we cannot observe how many chess pieces are on the customer's side. We also can't see the talents and preferences of those figures. Our competitors are playing on the same board, yet we know little about them. From time to time, new figures will appear on the board and some figures will disappear.

FIGURE 4-3

Ilustration of our experience of undiscovered account. Dark and foggy chessboard with unknown chess figures.

We have little control over this. Our main job is to position each figure in our company in the best spot on the game board, providing guidance and responsibility. The situation is always changing, yet knowledge about the customer is always relevant. The account plan will assist us to read the board better. It will give us perspective. The key is to see the full picture and use time as a resource. We should not ask colleagues to do things they cannot do, but position them at the right time and place to do their best.

"The expert in battle seeks his victory from strategic advantage and does not demand it from his men."
-Sun Tzu, "The Art of War" [54]

Closing Deals

The most important outcome for account management activities is getting orders. In B2B sales, the decision is made by several people. Usually, there are about five people involved in the deal. In most cases, a customer has a time schedule to finish the project. They need to purchase the necessary goods or services to finish the project. There is a countdown for every deal. Our job as an account manager is to allocate all the decisionmakers and steer them toward our solution. We have to do that before the time ends.

Neglecting one or more of the decisionmakers may cost us the deal. If we neglect the purchasing manager, he may support our competitor at the end of the negotiations. The technical expert may block us even if our prices are better. A manager will want to know how our solution saves the customer time and money.

Account managers usually set meetings with their friends (advocates of our product). Many salespeople prefer not to spend time with a customer who speaks against our solution. This is a big mistake. Salespeople should work on flipping them over. Others may assume the purchasing department is not as important as the R&D team. While this may be true, a purchasing manager can destroy us at the last moment. We will seldom succeed if we talk only to one person. It is like if we are playing chess and focusing only on the bishop and forgetting the rest of the class figures.

Remember, we will get the deal when all the decisionmakers choose us over our competitors.

Chapter Summary

All the pre-work described in this chapter leads us to a point where we can play the chess game. Mapping the account helps us to see most of the customer's figures and their positions. Preparing the purchasing list helps us understand the potential and mix of products. Block diagrams and solution descriptions give us an understanding of the problem our team needs to solve.

Now we need to position all our figures in the right spots. We must be honest about our team member's talents and character. Each one should be positioned in the right place at the right time. We must collect information and adjust the positions of our team on the chessboard accordingly. We should act based on the full picture, using time as a resource.

We know the timeline of each deal. We allocate and work with all decisionmakers. By the time the decision is made, most of the decisionmakers will be on our side.

To remember the concepts in this chapter, visualize a chessboard with figures of real people. Add some fog and competitors. Position each chess piece in the right spot.

FIGURE 4-4

Image of a chessboard with different figures, plans, moves, competition and uncertainty representing the work of an account manager with complex accounts.

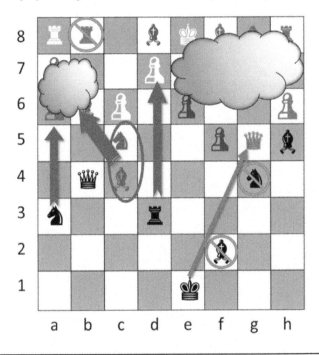

Chapter 5

The power of a community – Regional Community manager

"Of all the means which are procured by wisdom to ensure happiness throughout the whole of life, by far the most important is the acquisition of friends."
-Epicurus, Principal Doctrines [55]

We are all social beings. Although humans are undisputed rulers of this planet, we push ourselves to live in dense living conditions. According to the Global Rural-Urban Mapping Project (GRUMP) studies in 2010, cities occupy less than 3% of the available land on the planet (excluding Antarctica and Greenland). Moreover, based on a study published in 2014 in Landscape Ecology of Springer *(How Much of the World's Land has been Urbanized, Really? Hierarchical Framework for Avoiding Confusion,* A Z Liu, C He, Y Zhou, J Wu), the global built-up area is about 0.65 % in 2010, and the global impervious surface area is much smaller (about 0.45 %). [56] **Figure 5-1** taken from the article illustrates this very well.

FIGURE 5-1

Estimates of the world's urban land based on the newly-proposed nested hierarchy of urban definitions: [57]

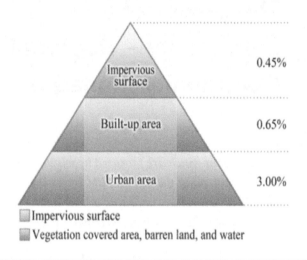

Impervious surface refers to human-made land covers through which water cannot penetrate, including rooftops, roads, driveways, sidewalks, and parking lots.

Built-up area its urban area dominated by non-vegetated, human-constructed elements such as roads, buildings, runways, and industrial facilities.

Urban area a is the total area within the administrative boundaries of a city, including all the impervious surfaces, vegetated areas, barren land, and water bodies.

According to Population Division of the United Nations Department of Economic and Social Affairs (UN DESA), In 2018, 55% of the world's population lived in urban areas, a proportion that is anticipated to increase to 68% by 2050. The most urbanized regions in 2018 were America (81%) and Europe (74%). In 2018, about 4.2 billion people resided in cities. According to estimations, this number will grow to 6.7 billion by 2050.[58]

There are different reasons why people choose to migrate to cities—occupation opportunities, medical care, better education, culture and more. Humans value these much more than the evils prevalent in a big city. Crime, epidemics, congestion, mental stress, and other city flaws are tolerated by us so we can enjoy big city life. It is a statistical fact that humans prefer high-density settlements.

Our ability to cooperate on a large scale combines millions of people executing different functions in society. This is exactly what a city enables us to do. In such a dense environment, each one of us can focus on their intrinsic worth. A doctor can be just a doctor. He doesn't need to clean his house. A cook can be just a cook. He does not need to be a driver, too. Cities provide us with variety of occupations to fulfill our physical and mental needs.

Because of the enormous number of people in the city, each individual can take part in different groups. While in a small village a person goes to a village church on Sunday to socialize, in a large city he has a variety of choices and communities.

Being part of something is in our nature. We even define ourselves through the communities in which we are active. A youngster who didn't find his place in one of the groups at school (cheerleaders, sport team members, musicians, or geeks) may experience depression. In the old times, exile was a severe punishment compared only to death.

Each one of us feels a mixture of different interests and beliefs. We are citizens of a country. We are engineers and salespeople. We are fans of a sports team. We are Christians or Muslims. We are family members. Each one of us feels unique and fulfilled as he picks his own path and finds good people with whom to share this path.

The development of the internet empowered people to find expressions for their uniqueness by joining online communities. Members of these communities subscribe to different forums and channels on social media platforms. There are communities with millions of people who consume content and follow community leaders. It is simple to search and join such groups. Just a few clicks and we are part of a unique worldwide international community.

Online communities are growing fast. Yet, as we consider the data, it makes us wonder. More than four billion people live in cities and the built-up area is just 0.65% of the surface of the plant. Humans are literally living on top of each other in large buildings to enjoy the same public space.

The high density and a variety of people in a big city is a perfect place for local specialized communities to thrive. At such density, it is possible to have in-person events about any specialized topic. We can build a community around a specific subject and have a monthly meeting with 80% of the members attending. It is a local physical community as opposed to an online community. Each church or synagogue has a local community. A fitness center is a local community. A local community no doubt has an online presence, as well, enabling information sharing, scheduling events, advertising and more. If enough people with the same narrow interest are living within a one-hour commute radius, wouldn't it be wonderful to meet them in person?

There is great joy in spending time with people who share your interests and values.

"Friends are as companions on a journey, who ought to aid each other to persevere in the road to a happier life."
-Pythagoras of Samos [59]

During the Covid-19 virus outbreak in 2020, many organizations submitted work from home policies, as this was imposed by governments. Many local communities such as churches and schools reinvented themselves online. It was a rapid adaptation. It looked as if the developed world could move entirely online. On the media during the lockdown, some voices speculated that people would move to the online way of life and city life would end. They said that humans would work from home, buy online and socialize through conference calls.

I cannot agree with those statements.

As soon as social distancing restrictions were lifted people were eager to get out and meet their friends and family. Children were waiting for schools to open so they could meet with their friends. Bars and restaurants were crowded and the hotels were overbooked. We learned that much work can be done remotely. We also learned about the strong human need for social interaction.

Our cities are historical monuments for human social necessity. Varanasi, Yanshi, Beirut, Luxor and Jerusalem are more than 5000 years old. Damascus, Byblos, Susa and Athens are more than 7000 years old. The plagues will pass and cities will hold up and grow.

As we discuss the idea of a local community, let us look at it through a business perspective. In the following points, we will consider common practices and suggest a new approach to improve customer engagement and sales.

Local Sales and Marketing Organization

Online commercial activity is constantly growing and probably will continue to grow every year. Technology enables customers to evaluate products and build personal relationships online. Perhaps, virtual reality may partly substitute for face-to-face interactions in the future. Yet today, face-to-face interaction is critical for building trust. Selling complex products or services cannot be done without trust. In general, trust between people is established by direct, in-person human interaction.

This is why large corporations hire local sales representatives in each region to facilitate this direct human interaction. Local salespeople are expected to have onsite meetings, lead product evaluations and deal with complex negotiations. Local salespeople are usually called regional sales managers, regional account managers, country managers or distribution channel managers, yet they all fulfill similar functions.

There is another manager who is in charge of the same region. Marketing managers have overlapping regions with sales managers. They hold the responsibility of driving marketing activities in the same regions. Company management usually disconnects those two functions in the organization. They see marketing as a lead generation tool and sales as a lead closing tool. Typically, marketing and sales have different metrics, targets, and management. VP Sales and VP Marketing report to the CEO as a part of the deployment of a worldwide strategy. VP Marketing leads advertising, creates awareness, builds online communities, and generates leads. VP Sales handles sales. It makes sense on the corporate level.

Local Specialized Community

A local community is a community where most of its members are living or working nearby. It could be a neighborhood or a church community. It may be a community of a certain golf club or fitness center members. The local community may have an online presence. It can be part of a much wider chain of communities sharing similar values, yet it is local. Thus, a local community enables people to meet other members in person. Unlike online communities, where people socialize by writing posts and sharing videos, local community members shake hands and have cocktail parties.

Our customers are part of many local communities in their private lives. Are they also members of professional communities? They probably are. Those kinds of communities may be a gold mine for a sales organization.

The following analysis is of the Israeli high-tech market in 2019. According to different studies in Israel, there are about 300,000 people working in the high-tech industry. Israel is a small country (similar to a big city in the US or Europe), so those people are less than 1.5 hours away from each other.

Let's imagine that we are regional sales managers of a large silicon component company addressing the Israeli market. We know that out of 300,000, only 1.5 thousand are potential customers. Most of the Israeli high-tech employees are developing software or silicon components. Our target audience is hardware engineers who are involved in developing electronic boards and electronic systems, so we need to focus on 0.5% of the industry to promote our products. It is likely those board designers are members of different professional communities and most of them are subscribed to online knowledge hubs and professional forums.

Are they part of local board design community—a community where they can communicate with people they know and can meet in person? Would those people like to be part of such a community?

I believe they would like to take an active part in such a community if it will benefit them.

How will Our Customers Benefit from such a Community?

Local professional communities give access to technical knowledge, business opportunities, talents, and occupational opportunities. Such a community may lead to research cooperation between several companies. People who left for other companies will find comfort in meeting their former friends at community events. It is a great place to recruit new talents at unofficial assemblies. Other members may be seeking experienced mentors, someone who could help them choose the right professional path. Senior members may be interested in giving back to society by teaching and consulting. Many members will even find new friends.

What will our Company Gain from the Community?

Facilitation of a local community will cost money and resources, but our company may be willing to invest in itself by starting a new community or positioning its people as key members of an existing community. I think those investments will pay off multiple times. Product marketing managers can learn about local market trends and the moods of the people who are driving the market. The introduction of new products and services will be much more efficient based on honest feedback from the community. Marketing managers will also gain from the segmentation which the specialization of the communities provide. Members of the community are part of the 0.5% of the industry to whom we should market our product. Community members will be open to receiving our marketing communication if it circulates within the community.

Sales managers will learn about new projects just from small-talk during social meetings. Salespeople can easily build relationships in an unofficial enticement. C-level managers may be much more receptive to discussing business with members of the community.

As our company supports the specialized community, it will create brand loyalty among community members. Strong brand loyalty will open doors for new customers. The community will be a commercial asset for our company.

Finally, organizations may contribute to society through philanthropy.

Who should be Responsible for a Local Community?

To address this, I suggest a new job title in a sales organization. This is the role of an LCM, a Local Community Manager. The job requirements of this person should:

- Join, build, and develop a community of customers around a common topic relevant to our offering.

- Become one of the leading members of the community by participation and providing value.
- Support social platforms: Facebook, YouTube, LinkedIn, cocktail parties, technical lectures, retreats, online forums and more.
- Recruit new members to join the community.
- Leverage the power of the community to promote our company's business activities: Product introductions, information about a new project, connection to management, finding new candidates and more.
- Build strong brand loyalty.

The LCM must be an active member of the community. He cannot just be a facilitator. People may not trust him, and he won't understand their needs. Participating in a community is being part of a special group with unique attributes. People won't follow us if we don't share ideas with them and have relevant knowledge and experience. We should be part of them.

Therefore, if the community is based around analog chip design, the LCM must be related to the analog chip design. If the community is based around cybersecurity, we must find a cyber lady to be our LCM. This person should be well acknowledged by other members. She should be able to attract people for interaction and have meaningful conversations with members of the community.

On the other hand, to keep this activity focused on company goals, we must choose a business-oriented person to manage this effort. The LCM's vision must align with long-term company interests.

As we are dealing with limited resources, it may be difficult to dedicate a full-time local person to this task. Moreover, a dedicated person may feel disconnected from company goals. Over time, a community manager may feel more committed to the community than to the long-term goals of the company. Therefore, I suggest the job of the local community managers be done by an experienced member of the sales team.

Local community management is like account management. We must deal with relationships and expectations and support the needs of the members of the community. Community management also requires some marketing activities. At its core, it is a personal, direct, and local activity. Therefore, a member of the sales organization should lead this effort.

Who in our team should do the extra work?

Should it be an account manager?
Young salesperson?
Sales manager?

Community members are key decisionmakers influencing our sales in the short and long run. They are our network of customer relationships and connections. Winning the trust of those people is a strategic task for the local sales team. Since this role may have a high impact on the bottom line, I suggest an experienced salesperson with an outgoing personality. It may be the regional sales manager or the second in line to manage the region. An experienced channel manager with a background in direct sales will also be a good candidate.

If the LCM job is done correctly, it will bring a lot of personal connections and friendships to the organization, assets that will help the LCM leverage his skills and promote inside the organization. Over time, the LCM will know key decisionmakers, VPs and CEOs relevant to our business. He may influence the market attitude toward our company's brand. The LCM plays an important role in the local sales organization, and he will gain much from this role.

Therefore, we need to choose wisely. The LCM must be a committed employee with a clear growth plan in our company. If we choose the wrong person or don't properly cultivate him, he may leave our company. If the LCM moves to our competitor, he will take many relationships with him. This will have a negative effect on our position in the community. The LCM role should be given to a loyal member of the sales organization, someone we plan to develop, promote, and keep for a long time. We need to acknowledge that it will take about 10%-20% of the sales manager's time to be the LCM. Part of his former responsibilities must be split between other members of the sales team.

How Do You Start and Develop a Local Community?

Each market, region and time are different. Something that is relevant to one culture will not be relevant to others. I hope the following steps will help you think about the challenge:

1. Who are the most important local decisionmakers of products or services? Profession, academic background, social and economic background, seniority, age and more.

2. What is the common denominator for those people in our region?

3. Look into similar local communities that address the same people.

4. Consider taking part in those communities and invest resources to position our people in key roles. We can then steer those communities in the right direction.

5. If there are no communities that address our market segment, we can start a new community.

6. What is the new community all about?

7. What might community members gain from this community?

8. Meet with potential key members and understand their point of view about your analysis.

9. Find local partners who might be interested in developing the community with us.

10. Prepare a yearly plan and allocate a budget. The plan should include aspects such as community events, community activities, finding sponsors and partners,

recruiting key members, online content, creating communication platforms, training and more.

If these appear to be general guidelines, let's take an example from the real world. Let's assume we are the sales managers of power modules for electronics hardware customers.

1. Who are the most important local decisionmakers of products or services? Profession, academic background, social and economic background, seniority, age and more.

    Electronics engineers developing electronics boards in high tech companies, mostly focusing on analog, power, and board design. In the majority, they will be experienced engineers in their late 30s and 40s. They are members of a team or team managers, but seldom will we find C-level managers deciding about power models.

2. What is the common denominator for those people in our region?

    - *Hardware design of electronic boards and analog circuits.*
    - *Analog and power design.*
    - *Signal and power integrity.*

3. Look into similar local communities that address the same people.

After some investigation, we found a power electronics seminar running every year. We noticed that some people participate every year. Most of them are relevant to our offering.

4. Consider taking part in those communities and invest resources to position our people in key roles. Then we can steer those communities in the right direction.

The power electronics seminar is a good place to start. It doesn't address all our customers, perhaps 25% of our potential customers. We can take an active part in arranging this event. We can also make several smaller events for the same audience. We can open an online forum and news list for those people. Together with the organizers of the event, we can build a community around the event. This will help us bring more people to the community.

5. If there are no communities that address our customers, we can start a new community.

Let's assume that we decided to develop a new community from scratch.

6. What is the new community all about?

Power design for electronic engineers.

7. What might community members gain from our community?

- *Technical knowledge*
- *Unbiased consulting with community members*
- *Finding coaches*
- *Job opportunities or talent recruitment*

8. Meet with potential key members and understand their point of view about your analysis.

   We need to meet with leading power designers who are working at leading companies and get honest feedback.

9. Find a local partner who might be interested in developing a community.

   We'll find a partner in sales and marketing organizations of companies operating with complementary products. Local distributors may be interested in this, as well. The professional local magazine already has a crowd of readers. They may be interested in organizing an event or running online workshops. They are always seeking for advertising budgets and quality content.

   Academia is a good place to find partners. Colleges and universities are interested in connecting with the industry. Those connections help universities be updated with industry needs. This accelerates finding the occupation process for their graduates.

10. Prepare a yearly plan and allocate a budget. The plan should include aspects such as community events, community activities, finding sponsors, recruiting

members, online content, creating communication platforms, training and more.

Prepare a plan with a budget, schedule and KPIs. Present the plan to management. Involve marketing at an early stage.

Chapter Summary:

In B2B sales, companies have challenges to build relationships with key decisionmakers. Salespeople invest time and effort to have direct interaction with those customers. Marketing runs online activities to increase demand for our products, yet marketing online activities seldom generate face-to-face interaction with key decisionmakers.

Our customers may be interested in taking part in the local professional community. In those communities, customers may find coaches, jobs, training, and friends. For us, a local professional community is a great way to build relationships with important customers and create brand loyalty.

We must assign a strong member of a sales team to lead a company relationship with such a community, a Local Community Manager (LCM). The LCM should take a leading part in the community and promote the commercial interests of our company.

For us to better remember the ideas presented in this chapter, I would like to share with you the following visual concepts to memorize:

Imagine a crowded room, a warm cocktail party of a professional community. People are laughing, sharing, and helping each other. As people mingle, you cannot know the organizations at which they work nor their positions there. In the middle of the room, you see your sales manager. He is radiating with charisma, talking to everyone, and introducing people. He is part of the community, yet he also orchestrated the event. The camera zooms out and you see a large logo of your company above his head. Then the camera zooms out more and you see that all members have logos above their heads. Some logos are big, some are small. Since our sales manager has a dominant role in the community, the logo of our company appears to be bigger than the rest.

Chapter 6

Effective and Antifragile sales organization

It happened before we knew the term COVID-19…

"I don't think the Paracetamol pills have any effect on me. I've never felt that way before. Can you call for a doctor? I think we should go to the hospital," whispered my wife.

"Honey, I'm afraid it may be the "swine flu" H1N1. Let's go to the hospital. I'm afraid for the baby. You are in your sixth month of pregnancy. This illness is not a joke. I'm calling your parents. Someone needs to stay with Keyla. We can't take her to the hospital. She is four years old."

During the winter of 2018 in the midst of Israeli's flu season, we had a swine flu outbreak and many people got sick. My wife was in the sixth month of pregnancy and probably caught the flu from one of her US clients. I decided not to take a chance and we drove to the nearest hospital, Sheba Medical Center. Sheba Medical Center has a dedicated maternity emergency room separate from the general emergency room. It has excellent dedicated medical staff and cutting-edge technology. Moreover, in 2020, *Newsweek* published its *Best Hospitals in the World* edition and ranked Sheba Medical Center as one of the top nine hospitals in the world. Sheba Medical Center shares the hall of fame with such names as Mayo Clinic - Rochester (US), Singapore General Hospital and Charite - Universitaetsmedizin Berlin. Strong proof of management and medical excellence. [60]

As we arrived at the hospital at 9pm, we experienced something totally different than what we'd anticipated. The maternity emergency room was crowded with people. Women in labor were sitting around the reception desk crouching in pain. There were no available delivery rooms to receive them. Some women had the flu, some had pregnancy-related medical issues, and some were progressing in giving birth. Their husbands, who looked as if they were suffering much more than the women themselves, were putting tremendous pressure on the reception nurses.

One reception nurse was standing in front of her computer and typing something with shaking hands. She was trying not to scream at the patients, but it was too much for her. As women cried, husbands and nurses shouted at each other.

After two hours, my wife felt even worse and asked me to take her home. Yet, we could not do that. According to hospital rules, once a patient signs in at the front desk, only a doctor can release her home. Otherwise, the visit may not be covered by insurance. Another hour passed and we lost hope of seeing a doctor. All we could do was sit huddled on a metal bench together with many other pregnant women and wait.

Three and a half hours passed until we saw the nurse, who connected my wife to the *Pinard horn* (Doppler ultrasound monitor). It took her some time since two out of three available monitors were broken. My wife was burning up with fever and the monitor showed moderate birth contractions, which is not a positive sign during the sixth month of pregnancy. The nurse could not provide her with any medicine or treatment since the doctor was not available to approve it. Finally, after four and a half hours, we were lucky enough to meet with a doctor. The doctor recommended hospitalizing my wife at once to provide her with urgent medical treatment and supervised bed rest. The hospital computer was broken, so the doctor could not submit the prescriptions for Celestone injections. We went back to the reception nurse, only to learn that there was no room for my wife in the overpopulated Pregnancy Retention Department. Only the unprecedented persuading power of my pregnant wife helped her to get a temporary hospital bed. In the end, she spent eight hours on a metal bench and for 48 hours did not get any treatment for her condition. But this is not how the story ends…

Two months after that, we rushed to the same maternity emergency room for an unplanned and urgent cesarean section operation. My wife had learned from her last experience, so she was mentally and physically prepared. We took a supply of medicine and food from home. In addition, we took some pillows, expecting to spend the night on the metal bench. But we were surprised again.

The same reception nurse met us at the same desk. This time, she was not shouting, but smiling. The computer and the equipment were working. After less than an hour, we saw a doctor and got a room. A few hours after that, one of the best doctors in the Sheba Hospital Center performed a successful cesarean section and we met our second daughter. My wife called it, "A wonderful experience."

What was the difference between the first and the second visit to the Sheba Medical Center? It was the same medical staff, the same management, and the same equipment. The difference was the number of patients. During our second visit, there were a substantial number of patients in the maternity emergency room, yet the emergency room was not overwhelmed. The medical staff was working hard but they were able to keep up with the pace. The technicians had sufficient time to fix or replace any broken equipment. The patients and their partners did not put stress on the nurses. They experienced slow but steady progress, so they remained calm.

In this story, the difference between a working system and a broken system is directly related to the number of patients waiting in the emergency room. Let's assume the emergency room can process 20 patients per hour. If there are 25 patients per hour, they can make it with some stress. If the number of patients per hour rises to 30, however, the system will break down. By *break down*, I mean the emergency room will not be able to process even 20 people per hour. Efficiency decreases dramatically with every new patient.

In the story above, we can see that the emergency room did not just work at a slower pace. We witnessed issues at many levels which led to other issues in a snowball effect.

- Patients with viral diseases were kept in proximity to a pregnant woman in the emergency room.
- Spouses and partners of patients were putting a lot of stress on the front desk nurse.
- The front desk nurse could not focus on her tasks— prioritizing medical cases, inviting technicians to fix equipment, and coordinating with Pregnancy Retention Department.
- Equipment was not working properly, creating false readings and more delays.
- Doctors and nurses could not do their work with broken equipment and computers.
- Patients in pain with different medical conditions (some urgent) could not get treatment.

An important question is why the system breaks instead of just slowing down? Why did the emergency room nurses not limit themselves to 25 patients per hour?

Because they cannot. A maternity emergency room cannot just say to a woman in labor that she cannot get treatment. The medical staff must receive all patients and start working on their cases.

If the same situation happened in a production line in a factory, then we could just slow down the production line. This would reduce piles of inventory and give the technical staff time to fix the equipment. Another root of action is implemented by amusement parks. An overcrowded amusement park will just close its gates for a while. It may upset the kids at the gate, but it will keep the waiting lines short for the customers who are already inside. Ethernet communication adopted a similar approach. Ethernet routers have memory buffers that can hold a certain amount of Ethernet packets. If the number of packets in the queue is too big, the Ethernet router just drops packets. Those routers won't collapse. It will just process the maximum number of packets at its full capacity and erase the rest.

Hospitals can't use those techniques. Emergency rooms cannot erase patients, nor can it close its doors. Patients will just keep coming through the front door, so this system can break. It is a fragile system.

In his book *Antifragile*, Professor Nassim Taleb gave a good definition of fragility and antifragilety. *Fragility* is a concave sensitivity to stressors, causing a negative sensitivity to an increase in volatility. [61] In other words, the system has a strong nonlinear response to a strong stressor.

Antifragility was defined by Nassim Taleb as a convex response to a stressor or source of harm (for some range of variation), leading to a positive sensitivity to increase in volatility (or variability, stress, dispersion of outcomes, or uncertainty, what is grouped under the designation *disorder cluster*). [63]

In **Figure 6-1** we can observe a linear line (A) describing harm to a system from a certain event. The linear line may describe closed gates of an amusement park or a dropping of Ethernet packets by an Internet router. An overflow (stress) of a hundred packets will cause a drop of a hundred packets. An overflow of a thousand packets will cause the router to drop a thousand packets. A linear response would be a represented by a linear function $Y(x) = a*X + C$.

The nonlinear line (B) represents a system that will break at some point. When the stressor effect is low, this line appears linear. As the stress effect grows, the harm to the system likewise grows at a rapid pace. Like in emergency rooms, 24 patients per hour will cause one hour of extra waiting time, but 30 patients per hour will cause four extra hours of waiting time and many cases of false medical diagnoses. Line B in **Figure 6-1** represents fragility.

FIGURE 6-1

Disproportionate effect of tail events on nonlinear exposures, illustrating the necessary character of the nonlinearity of the harm function and showing how we can extrapolate outside the model to probe unseen fragility. Source: Authors. Mathematical Definition, Mapping, and Detection of (Anti)Fragility, Nasim Taleb. [62]

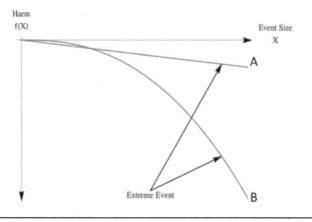

Line A is a linear line, representing systems that can handle stress without breaking down.

Line B is a nonlinear line, representing systems that can handle minor stress, yet it will break down under strong stressors. Stressors have a nonproportional, accelerating negative effect on those systems.

An emergency room cannot cope with all possible scenarios. The COVID-19 virus with thousands of patients will definitely overwhelm it. A hospital can prepare their facilities to deal with the seasonal flu, so an emergency room may be Antifragile or Robust to seasonal flu, although it will break under the burden of an epidemic.

Almost every system has a breaking point. The problem is that we don't know to what extent our system is robust and when it will become fragile. The biggest challenge is to find the breaking point of the system. A breaking point is a point at which the response to stressors is no longer linear but is exponential. This knowledge helps managers push the organization to the limit but keep it away from the breaking point.

All commercial companies are optimized to be extremely efficient. Companies implement different methods to reduce resources in their processes, methods including the Toyota Production System, the Theory of Constringes, Agile, Just-in-time and more. Companies fight to save costs, implement automation, reduce inventory and working capital, increase financial leverage and improve logistics. Some companies have profit formulas that lead them to cut personnel and reduce investments in R&D to improve their financial reports.

This makes them more fragile to volatility in sales, the supply chain and time to market. Perhaps after the crises we've experienced with the COVID-19 virus, companies will change their methodologies, yet I believe after some time, the crisis will be forgotten and we will go back to our old ways.

Let us see how this applies to sales organizations. Sales is a high volatility activity. There is a lot of uncertainty in the selling process. Sales are affected by different market factors:

- Yearly seasonality
- New product introduction
- Competitive product introduction
- Market growth
- Distribution and end customer stocking levels
- Nature disasters and epidemics
- Negative publicity
- Geopolitical changes
- Changes in regulation and taxation

These factors may dramatically increase or decrease sales. External factors are stressors to the sales organization, which may lead to system break down. For example, changes in taxation may lead to a strong decrease in sales, which would lead to demoralization and layoffs. Eventually, the best salespeople may choose to leave the company for our competition.

A strong increase in sales may also disrupt sales and customer service organizations. Overwhelmed salespeople will have trouble addressing all potential opportunities, so market share will be lost to competition. Customer service will be underwater over a large number of cases and complaints. Besides bad publicity, unhappy customers will call salespeople to complain. As a result, salespeople will deal with complaints, putting more pressure on customer service. Eventually, this may lead to missed opportunities and poor yearly performance. If this happens during the hot season, it will have a devastating effect on yearly revenue. A sales process is not a production line process. There are peaks and there are lows. In many cases, one good month can make a bad year into a good year. A certain deal can bring more revenue than the entire year of work. Missing those peaks is a system breakdown in sales.

Therefore, for the sales team to be robust or antifragile is to be able to adjust to rapid changes in market demand. Sales organizations must be flexible!

What do I mean by flexibility in sales?

A famous example of flexibility in sales is demonstrated through a story about a taxi driver. A taxi driver is willing to work for eight hours per day, every day. His target is to earn $200 per day. As soon as the taxi driver reaches his target, he is pleased and goes home to his family. Some days are very rainy, and people prefer to use a taxi. On rainy days, the taxi driver reaches his target after working just four hours. He earns $50 per hour. After achieving his target in four hours, the driver spends the rest of the day at home.

There are sunny days, as well. On those days, people prefer to walk or ride a bicycle. Sunny days are bad days for the taxi driver. He spends many hours cruising around looking for customers. On those days, he reaches his target after 12 hours of hard and unsatisfying work. Then the taxi driver goes to sleep without spending quality time with his family.

By doing simple math, we can see that it is much more beneficial for the taxi driver to work 12 hours on the rainy days and spend the sunny days with his family.

As an example, let's assume that the number of sunny days and the rainy days are equal, and each working day has only 12 hours. We can calculate taxi driver benefits from both strategies over one year:

Original strategy — Work hard to reach the target.
Yearly Revenue: 365 days x $200 = $73,000
Hours spent with family per year:
365days/2 x (12 hours-4 hours) + 365days/2 x (12 hours - 12 hours) = 1,460 hours

Smart Strategy — Work hard on rainy days strategy:
Yearly Revenue: 365days/2 x (12 hours x $50) = $109,500
Number of hours spent with family per year:
365days/2 x (12 hours) + 365days/2 x (12 hours - 12 hours) = 2190 hours

This simple example illustrates an important concept of flexibility in sales. By adopting to market conditions, the taxi driver earned $36,500 more and yet spent 730 more hours enjoying quality time with his family. It is exactly 50% more free time and 50% more money.

Sure, you would say: "This is intuitive! It is rational! We act exactly the same in our company."

Really... Are we?

In most sales organizations today we have quarterly, monthly and weekly predetermined targets. Even in bad times, sales managers expect the salespeople to reach their predetermined targets, so during bad times, frustrated salespeople work 24/7 just to survive. During the good times, targets stay the same, so salespeople are happy to reach their targets and relax. Salespeople may think, "Who knows what tomorrow will bring? This month, I reached my target. I can go home and relax." If this salesperson is acting irrationally, it is only because of the compensation structure and his job insecurity.

If a salesperson gets a new quota each year, it is a non-cumulative function. At the beginning of each year, he starts from zero and works hard to reach his quota, so if he reaches his quota in November, the salesperson can rest easy in December. In January he will get a new target for the year. Sales targets are non-accumulative—they start from zero each year.

However, this is not the case with company revenue and profit. Revenue and profit are accumulative functions. The company doesn't start from zero each year. The revenue is invested in R&D, sales operations, and infrastructure. Those investments create a long-term accumulative effect and a competitive advantage. Therefore, it is strategic for organizations to keep the salespeople extremely motivated during the good times.

The inability to adapt to market conditions is common on the organizational level, as well. Most sales organizations don't have a clear priority mechanism for sales managers. For example, during good times, sales directors may be focusing on testing the market for a new unproven product. What the sales director should be doing during the good times is keeping salespeople running like crazy and collecting orders for proven products. But sales managers are bound to prioritize new experimental products based on the yearly plan. If the sales organization cannot adjust to market conditions, it is fragile.

Flexibility is about resource allocation and deployment. Most sales organizations don't have flexible structures. This means they cannot move people quickly to support booming demands in hot markets. This is fragility.

For example, the automotive market may experience a certain slowdown just as the demand in the defense market may be strong. In this case, it would be wise to temporarily allocate resources to support the defense market. A company that has a flexible team of sales engineers, inside sales and customer support and can quickly move them is antifragile. Not every company can do that.

Many organizations are fragile to change because their area sales directors aren't able to act fast enough. The first reason they cannot act fast is the lack of clarity on sales organization priorities. In many cases, companies fail to provide a simple and transparent set of priorities.

Yes, money is the king! Agreed, revenue comes first. But what is important after that? Is it market share or high margin? Should sales directors ask salespeople to push new products or focus on solution-based selling? Is new customer acquisition more important than our key customer satisfaction?

If someone says *all of the above* is important, then I would say, "Then...let us be focused on everything." Lack of clear priorities creates confusion and inability to react fast to market changes.

The second reason for the inability of sales directors to quickly refocus resources is fundamental. In many companies, resources (application engineers, marketing, service, operations) don't report to sales directors. In many companies, sales directors only manage salespeople, yet all the other functions have different managers. They have different KPIs (Key Performance Indicators) and different priorities, so even if the sales director is willing to quickly adapt, he cannot. He would need to get a lot of approvals from different managers. Meanwhile, we lose market share.

Absence of clear priorities and the inability to allocate resources prevents sales directors from quickly adjusting. As a result, we are fragile to market changes, which are so frequent in the modern world.

We spoke a lot about the fragility and challenges in sales organizations. It is not my intention to preach about the wickedness of sinners. It is easy to point out problems and discuss potential hazards. Instead, we should focus on finding solutions and processes to make our sales organizations less fragile and more robust. Let us discuss ways to make our organizations more efficient, adjustable and a bit more antifragile.

A Way to Efficiency and Antifragility

There may be a conflict between antifragility and efficiency. Efficient processes are optimized to make the most of available resources, leaving no slack and no redundancy in the system. On the other hand, antifragility is based on flexibility and endurance to market changes. Antifragile organizations improve their position and market share in extreme market conditions.

The conflict manifests in the difficulty to contract organizations that would be both efficient and adjustable to changes in market conditions at the same time. At business-as-usual times, a competitive organization needs to be as efficient as possible. During extremely good times, organizations must quickly scale up to maximize revenue and keep market share. During extremely bad times, organizations need to reduce costs and be flexible enough to refocus their resources.

"When we are no longer able to change a situation...we are challenged to change ourselves."
–Victor Emil Frankl [64]

Practically speaking, to become both efficient and antifragile, sales organizations need to implement the following changes:

1. Start with the best Information Technology (IT) system you can afford

"It is a capital mistake to theorize before one has data."
-Words of Sherlock Holmes, Conan Doyle. [65]

There are many resources for external data. We can order market research, talk to leading customers, or use academic studies. Yet, if we fail to collect and organize our own data, we are blind and foolish. Without precise and often updated data, all our conclusions are really just speculations. Data is critical both for efficiency and antifragility.

The first step is to define the most significant KPI (Key Performance Indicators) and measure them in an automatic, systematic, and repetitive way. It is vital to collect the data in the same way over a long period of time. This will give us the ability to compare data from different periods and market conditions. Therefore, as we engineer those systems, we must take into account our future needs. For example, actions such as moving products from one product family to another, changing currency or splitting regions will affect the way we collect data. This will prevent us from comparing yearly performance. As a result, we may fail to discover market trends.

An equally important role of Information Technology (IT) in organizations is the allocation of tasks and resources. For example, Marketing Qualified Leads (MQL) are assigned to salespeople by the CRM (Customer Relationship Management) systems. The customer support process is also managed in CRM. In some companies, advertising allocation and tracking is computer automated. A CRM sales funnel affects the deployment of application engineers. Effective IT systems must be flexible and easy to use. This will aid the organization in allocating resources on the fly as markets go through booms and busts.

2. Champagne Pyramid Model

The name is quite symbolic, as it is common for salespeople to party hard when times are good. To understand this concept, imagine a pyramid of champagne glasses on top of each other. Now let's assume that revenue is the champagne pouring from the top of the glass pyramid, creating a cascading waterfall. Our resources are the glasses forming the pyramid. The most effective resources are at the top layers of the pyramid. The lower level glasses represent less-effective resources in the sales organization. At the bottom of the waterfall are the least effective resources. **Figure 6-2** illustrates this concept.

FIGURE 6-2

Image of a pyramid of champagne glasses and pouring champagne. This image represents a principal for resources deployment based on business volume. [66]

By the most effective resources, I mean our superstar salespeople and other key contributors, people who have the best potential to win deals and convert the funnel to sales. Those people must be always occupied, fulfilled and well-compensated. The least effective resources may be untrained external call center employees who answering calls when we cannot. In the middle of the pyramid, we might find resources such as technical distributors, system integrators, junior salespeople, external technical subcontractors, and others.

Usually, there is not enough champagne in the waterfall to cascade down to fill the bottom of the pyramid, so only the top and the middle of the pyramid handles the business. When the market is booming, champagne overflows from the middle of the pyramid to the glasses at the bottom. When times are rough and business is slow, the top glasses will still be full, but there will not be enough business to fill the middle rows of the pyramid. Those resources can be quickly moved to support other markets or adjusted by working less hours.

The Champagne Pyramid model is an intuitive concept. Keeping this concept in mind will aid us in building an efficient and flexible organization.

We need to define and measure the volume of champagne in each glass at each level of the pyramid, which means measuring the capacity of our salespeople. We also need to decide when they are in an overflow mode so we may share the workload with lower levels of the pyramid. A simple solution may be to measure the revenue assigned to each salesperson. If an average deal is $50K and a salesperson can manage 200 deals per year, then he should be responsible for $1 million/year of revenue. In bad times, he may be 80% occupied, and in good times he may bring in $1.2M. In this case, to keep him working hard in good times, the organization must give him a *good times target*. A *good times target* should have incremental compensation for the salesperson. Demotivating salespeople during good times is a bad idea. During good times, we want our salespeople to be workaholics.

Revenue is an intuitive KPI for measuring salespeople's capacity, yet in real life, this is not so simple. Every business is different, and each salesperson is different. My personal indicator is the salesperson's number of visits to major accounts. If a salesperson does not have the necessary time to spend at each major account, then he is overwhelmed.

Setting priorities is a mandatory step in the implementation of the Champagne Pyramid concept.

Resource allocation cannot be down without a clear set of priorities. We need to specify organizational priorities and measure the resource capacity at each level of the pyramid. Our job as managers is to prioritize activities and then dynamically allocate resources based on the employee's capacity and market conditions.

A simple, clear, and unified set of priorities for the entire sales organization is key for coordination. This will keep everyone focused on the most important activities during all market conditions. Without clear and unified priorities, salespeople will be confused. Managers may dispute over resources. Directors may put their own interests before the good of the company.

Simple and clear priorities may be stated as that revenue is more important than margin, or we could state that we should focus on end customers more than on the distribution channel. We may prioritize frontal meetings over expenses reduction and so on. A simple chart or a few clear statements are sufficient for this task.

We should also apply the Champagne Pyramid concept to other functions and resources in our organization. Customer service, technical support and inside sales should be managed by the same principles. This approach gives clear and predetermined guidelines for all company managers on how to prioritize their resources. This approach will stand both booming and busting markets, helping to scale the organization fast and meet market requirements. This approach also gives the local leader sufficient power to adjust their organization without going through long approval processes.

3. Organizational Matrix Structure

In any sales organization, we have different functions working together to support customers and drive sales. Sales managers are responsible for a territory, market or lists of customers. Sales managers should know their territories and have plans on how they will grow the business. The core knowledge of the salespeople is the business knowledge of their territories. Therefore, if their territory is suffering from bad market conditions, it is inefficient to deploy them to another territory. Salespeople need to learn the new territory before they will be valuable contributors.

On other hand, there are technical support, customer service, telemarketing, and others who all support sales managers and customer-related activities. We may call valuable people *resources*. The core knowledge of those resources is more operational, technical or product specific. For example, presale engineers are familiar with company products and customer technical requirements. Customer service employees are good at solving customers problems. Those skills are technical and product-knowledge related rather than in-the-market related. Those skills may be applicable to different territories and customers. Therefore, those resources may be quickly deployed when and where they are needed the most. They are much more flexible than the salespeople, at least in the short run.

In order to maximize the antifragility of the sales organization, we can leverage the qualities mentioned above. In other words, we need to be able to dynamically allocate resources.

Matrix Organization Structure is the most effective structure to achieve dynamic resource allocation. In matrix structure, we will have salespeople indirectly managing resources in their territory. As the salesperson requires more resources, we allocate more resources to his territory.

To have both efficiency and antifragility, we need to react quickly to changes. This can be achieved by empowering the area sales director to manage all the resources in their region. It will give the area sales directors the flexibility to quickly react to market changes and reallocate resources. Otherwise, sales directors would have to get approvals from several managers to change deployment. This will lead to discussions, disputes, and a lack of action. We would not be able to react quickly enough to changing market conditions.

In **Figure 6-3** we see an example of Matrix Organization Structure implemented in a sales organization.

FIGURE 6-3

Typical Matrix Organization Structure implemented in a sales organization.

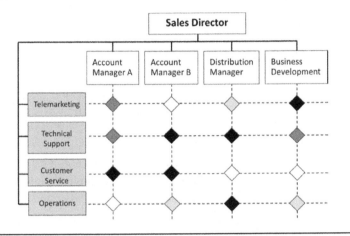

The sales director must carry the management burden of coordinating sales, marketing, service, and technical support. Therefore, the company should support the sales director with best IT systems and development of people possible. The area sales director could focus only on using muscles rather than building muscles. This will reduce management overhead and focus the sales organization on execution.

A combination of Organization Matrix Structure with the Champagne Pyramid Model provides the ability and flexibility to adjust quickly. With the right KPIs and clear priorities, we will know when and how to adjust to changes. This is sales organization antifragility. Each change that sales organization experiences will prepare it for future changes. Resources allocation to support multiple territories will improve. Salespeople will know how to capture maximum revenue as their territory booms. Sales managers learn to be tolerant when resources are focused elsewhere. The improvement of organizational ability to quickly adjust is antifragility.

Efficiency is another important goal which can be achieved by matrix structure. As each person focuses on a certain task, he can become an expert in his field. As our people become better at what they do, our organization becomes more efficient and effective.

In a matrix structure, resources can specialize in a certain technical field and support multiple salespeople. Although as the market changes and their efforts will be required in a different territory, their skills will still be relevant. Over time, they will become better at what they do, and we can call them experts. In vertical organization structure, an application engineer will support all applications in his territory, so he'll have a wider knowledge of multiple applications, yet it may be difficult for him to build deep expertise in a narrow field. In a matrix structure, he can specialize.

As we work within a matrix structure, resources split their time between several territories. In order to track sales organization efficiency, we have to measure where their time is spent. Otherwise, we may overinvest in somewhere and underinvest in another place. We may fail to spot underperforming markets or sales managers. Therefore, measurement of workload and the number of working hours is the key to reaching efficiency. Measurement of workload and capacity is also a major element in the Champagne Pyramid model. It is the main indicator for managers to increase capacity by deploying resources from the lower level of the Champagne Pyramid.

Measurement of workload in matrix organizations can be difficult. It requires some discipline from the employee to record their activities. We should do our best to leverage the technologies in our IT systems to reduce the unpleasant paperwork. Yet, this may be far from ideal.

We must also define a measuring unit for the workload so we can compare the workload of different resources. I think the key indicator of workload is the number of hours spent in a certain territory per month. The working hours of our people is a limited resource. As we will run out of time, we'll have to pay for external resources such as distributors, consultants, and telemarketing services. We can also build efficiency indicators by dividing revenue by hours or dividing funnel by hours. Therefore, measuring working hours of resources would be my tool of choice in the quest for efficiency.

There are different ways to measure working hours spent on different tasks. IT tools may be helpful in this task, yet in sales organizations, employees are distributed and spending much of their time at customer sites. Traveling and working nonstandard hours is part of sales organization DNA. I think eventually we'll have to count on the direct feedback of people working in the resource teams. People will just have to fill forms documenting how many hours they've spent on a certain sales territory.

This may also be tricky since people may exaggerate to make a point. Some may play with the numbers to seek their own gains, such as less traveling or a promotion. To overcome this, we can use a well-known statistical technique called *conjoint analysis.* Conjoint analysis is widely used to measure preferences for product features in marketing research. [67] This technique was developed by marketing professor Paul E. Green to get from customers their preferences. It helps researchers to extract information that customers may not know about themselves or would not intentionally share. In conjoint analysis, we build a multiple question survey. In each question, we ask the customer to price a different set of features. Using statistics, we can find a customer-preferred price for each separate feature, something that customers could not or would not provide if directly asked.

In our challenge of measuring working hours, we can build a conjoint analysis to learn about time invested in each territory by building a multiple question survey. Instead of price, we can ask employees to estimate invested working hours. Instead of features, we can use sales territories. Conjoint analysis, commonly used to analyze the price of a product feature, will give as the number of hours each resource invested in a certain sales territory.

There are many things we can do. I think **Table 6-1** is a good starting point for the sales director to analyze where our people are spending their time.

TABLE 6-1

Table for efficiency calculation and resource allocation.

		Account Manager A	Account Manager B	Distribution Manager	Business Development	Total Hours per Resource
	Sales Director					
Telemarketing	Caller 1	40	40	0	80	160
	Caller 2	0	0	120	40	160
	Total Telemarketing	40	40	120	120	320
Technical Support	Application Engineer	80	40	20	20	160
	Softwere Engineer	20	80	0	60	160
	Solution Architect	10	10	40	100	160
	Total Technical Support	110	130	60	180	480
Customer Service	Online Support	10	10	140	0	160
	System Service Engineer	60	60	40	0	160
	IT Service Engineer	40	80	40	0	160
	Total Customer Service	110	150	220	0	480
Operations	Booking Coardinatore	30	30	100	0	160
	Logistics Coordinator	80	70	0	10	160
	Logistics Coordinator	0	0	160	0	160
	Total Operations	110	100	260	10	480
Total Hours per Salesperson		370	420	660	310	
Total Funnel in $K per Salesperson		4,720	5,880	1,810	7,970	
Total Yearly sales in $K per Salesperson		2,250	2,950	4,250	550	

4. When there is No War to Fight, Prepare for One

"When fishermen cannot go to sea, they repair nets."
—Nabil Sabio Azadi [68]

Whatever the reason, we will have times when business is slow. It may be just one or two weeks during the summer vacation period. It could also be a much longer period as a result of natural disasters or geopolitical situations. It will happen, despite what we may do to be antifragile by using the Champaign Pyramid concept and Organization Matrix Structure. Based on the Champagne Pyramid concept, we will drive all our business through our best salespeople. We will stop using external resources that stand on lower levels of the pyramid model. Based on the Matrix Organizational Structure, we will allocate resources to territories where business is still strong, yet we will have unoccupied resources, just because, temporarily, the market is not there.

Even if our best salespeople work at 200% of their capacity, they won't not be able to get more than what the market has to offer. Remember the story about the taxi driver? Does it make sense to work 12 hours a day on a sunny day?

So, what should we do with our people and how should we measure their success?

During peacetime, the army is not sitting at home doing nothing. Soldiers are training, engineers are constructing weapons and intelligence is collecting information. The army is preparing for future action, and so should we.

Quiet times are bad for business, but they are opportunities to allocate time for building assets for the company. During those times, we could upgrade our CRM system and improve our processes. We should create marketing content. We might seek out new markets which were neglected in the past. We could also search for potential channel partners and subcontractors. We may have team building events and some relaxation time which we've postponed so many times. Every company should have a quiet times list of potential projects and the preapproved budget for their execution. Sales managers should become project managers, driving teams to execute projects on time, the same as military infantry officers manage logistics and prepare projects for the next assignment. Like the military infantry officers, we will have to manage preparation duties so our salespeople and equipment will be ready.

> *"If I had five minutes to chop down a tree, I'd*
> *spend the first three sharpening my axe."*
> *-Abraham Lincoln* [69]

The most important and significant project is to train and develop our people. Quiet times are the best possible times do to so. We must have a personalized training plan for an unforeseen business slowdown. Training and learning must be methodical and measurable. Training should have clear milestones with tests or projects. Without it, the organization will not be able to monitor the development of salespeople. Moreover, during this time, we can motivate salespeople by counting their training progress in their quota. If we sincerely believe that highly skilled salespeople are our main assets, we should put our money where our beliefs are.

> *" The nation that will insist on drawing a broad line*
> *of demarcation between the fighting man and the*
> *thinking man is liable to find its fighting done by*
> *fools and its thinking done by cowards."*
> *-Sir William Francis Butler* [70]

Our sales organization must have an action plan and set of priorities for the activities listed above. Otherwise, as those times arrive, sales organizations will be confused and demoralized.

Chapter Summary:

I believe that by implementing these models, sales organizations will become both efficient and adjustable. Efficient enough to maximize revenue with available resources and adjustable enough to adapt to changing market conditions to become to some extent antifragile.

Steps to take to make sales organization both efficient and antifragile to market conditions:

1. **Implement the Best IT System You can Afford.**

   Correct decisions and fast adjustments are based on precise data. Data acquisition should be automatic, repetitive, and consistent.

2. **Implement the Champagne Pyramid Model.**

   By monitoring the capacity of each level in the pyramid, we can scale up and down our organization, fitting the market demand. Our best people, the upper layers of the pyramid, will be occupied but not overwhelmed during all market conditions. To make this approach antifragile, we must predetermine each level capacity and monitor it with IT systems.

3. **Implement a Matrix Organization Structure for all Customer-Related Functions and Resources, Managed by the Sales Director.**

   Resources should be assigned to markets/ territories with maximum impact. The sales director must be empowered to deploy resources on the fly, harvesting the most profitable markets.

4. **Create Clear Priorities and KPIs for all Market Conditions.**

   Create a simple, clear, and transparent set of priorities and KPIs for the whole sales origination for all times. This will keep us continuously focused.

5. **Plan to Build Strength during Slow Periods.**

   Create a prioritized action plan with a list of projects executed by sales managers. The training and development of people is the most important activity, so it should be monitored and rewarded.

In **Figure 6-4** we can find a visual summary of this chapter.

FIGURE 6-4

Chapter 6 flowchart – Effective and Antifragile sales organization. This flowchart will help us remember the ideas of this chapter.

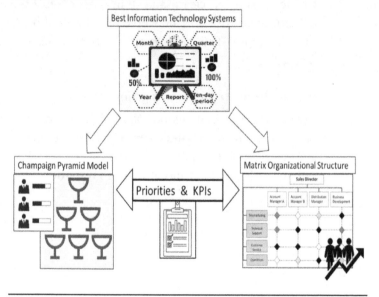

Summary

Dear reader,

Thank you for bearing with me through the entire book. I hope you found few ideas to serve you in your endeavors.

We humans have limited memory to recall facts and lists.

After a few weeks, you may not remember much of what is discussed in this book. That's okay. It is part of who we are. We are much better in remembering stories, symbols, places and walking trails. I tried to use those as memory anchors in this book.

In each chapter of this book, I've positioned emotional stories so you will remember what the chapter is all about. I've also created visual models at the end of each chapter which will help you to remember and implement the main idea of each chapter.

I really appreciate all your feedback, and I love hearing what you have to say. Please send me an email to the following address: sellosophy.ariel@gmail.com

I wish you the best!

Final Words

"It never ceases to amaze me: we all love ourselves more than other people, but care more about their opinion than our own. If a god appeared to us—or a wise human being, even—and prohibited us from concealing our thoughts or imagining anything without immediately shouting it out, we wouldn't make it through a single day.

That's how much we value other people's opinions—instead of our own."

-Marcus Aurelius [71]

About the Author

Ariel Feder (Feyderov) is a business development manager and a system engineer with more than 15 years of hands-on experience in the high-tech industry.

Ariel has worked with top organizations and startups in the Israeli high tech industry on leading technologies. Over the years, Ariel developed expertise in management, system engineering, pre/post-sales, and business development.

Ariel is passionate about creating efficient and effective organizations to fulfill the needs of all stakeholders. He believes that combining ideas from different disciplines into practical models is the main driver of business innovation. In his life and work, Ariel combines eastern and western philosophy, humanistic psychology, project management, engineering, and street smarts.

Ariel holds a master's degree in business and finance and a bachelor's degree in electronics engineering. He started his career serving in the technology department of the Israeli communication corps, at the rank of Captain.

References

1. Isaac Newton remarked in a letter to his rival Robert Hooke dated 5 February 1676 [O.S.][9] (15 February 1676 [N.S.]). Turnbull, H.W. ed., 1959. The Correspondence of Isaac Newton: 1661-1675, Volume 1, London, UK: Published for the Royal Society at the University Press. p. 416

2. Huai-Nan Tzu, and Thomas F Cleary. The Book of Leadership and Strategy : Lessons of the Chinese Masters. Kindle Edition ed., Boston, Shambhala ; [New York, 1992, p. 888.

3. Christensen, Clayton M, and Michael E Raynor. The Innovator's Solution : Creating and Sustaining Successful Growth. Boston, Massachusetts, Harvard Business Review Press, 2013, p. 73. note 3.

4. Levitt, Steven D, and Stephen J Dubner. Freakonomics. New York, Ny, Harpercollins Publishers Inc, 2005, p. 91.

5. Adamson, Brent, et al. The Challenger Customer : Selling to the Hidden Influencer Who Can Multiply Your Results. London, Portfolio Penguin, 2015.

6. Voss, Christopher, and Tahl Raz. Never Split the Difference : Negotiating as If Your Life Depended on It. London, Random House Business Books, 2017.

7. Godin, Seth. Tribes We Need You to Lead Us. 2014.

8. Thinking, Fast and Slow. 1 ed., New York, Farrar, Straus And Giroux, 25 Oct. 2011.

9. Cmglee. "English: Comparison of Probability Density Functions, p(k) for the Sum of n Fair 6-Sided Dice to Show Their Convergence to a Normal Distribution with Increasing n, in Accordance to the Central Limit Theorem. In the Individual Probability Distribution Functions, the Minima, Maxima and Mods Are Labelled. In the Bottom-Right Graph, Smoothed Profiles of the Previous Graphs Are Rescaled, Superimposed and Compared with a Normal Distribution, Shown in Black." Wikimedia Commons, commons.

   https://commons.wikimedia.org/wiki/File:Dice_sum_central_limit_theorem.svg Accessed 5 June 2020.

10. Hill, Napoleon. Think and Grow Rich : The Complete Classic Text. New York, N.Y., Jeremy P. Tarcher/Penguin, 2008.

11. Collins, Jim. Good to Great : Why Some Companies Make the Leap ... and Others Don't. London, Random House, 2001.

12. Kaplan, Justin, ed. (2002). "Reinhold Niebuhr (1892–1971)". Bartlett's Familiar Quotations (17th ed.). p. 735. (attributing the prayer to Niebuhr in 1943)

13. Eisenhardt, K.M. (1989), "Agency Theory: An Assessment and Review", The Academy of Management Review, 14 (1): 57–74

14. Mintzberg, Henry. "The Design School: Reconsidering the Basic Premises of Strategic Management." Strategic Management Journal, vol. 11, no. 3, Mar. 1990, pp. 171–195, 10.1002/smj.4250110302. Accessed 31 Aug. 2019.

15. Ansoff, H. Igor. "Critique of Henry Mintzberg's 'The Design School: Reconsidering the Basic Premises of Strategic Management.'" Strategic Management Journal, vol. 12, no. 6, Sept. 1991, pp. 449–461, 10.1002/smj.4250120605.

16. Carl von Clausewitz, Vom Kriege, Book 1, Chapter 3.

17. Tyson, Mike. "Everyone Has a Plan till They Get Punched in the Mouth. #miketyson #vintagetyson." Twitter, 18 Oct. 2018,

twitter.com/MikeTyson/status/1052665864401633299/photo/1.
Accessed 5 June 2020.

18. Wade, Nicholas. "The Scourge of Soviet Science." Wall Street
    Journal, 17 June 2016, www.wsj.com/articles/the-scourge-of-soviet-
    science-1466192179. Accessed 5 June 2020.

19. DeJong-Lambert, William (2017). The Lysenko Controversy as a
    Global Phenomenon, Volume 1: Genetics and Agriculture in the
    Soviet Union and Beyond. Palgrave Macmillan. p. 104

20. LI, C. C. "Lysenkoism in China." Journal of Heredity, vol. 78, no. 5,
    Sept. 1987, pp. 339–340, 10.1093/oxfordjournals.jhered.a110407.
    Accessed 5 Dec. 2019.

21. Karl Popper, Conjectures and Refutations, London: Routledge and
    Keagan Paul, 1963, pp. 33-39; from Theodore Schick, ed., Readings
    in the Philosophy of Science, Mountain View, CA: Mayfield
    Publishing Company, 2000, pp. 9-13.

22. Mya Tin, Daw, and Central University Of Tibetan Studies. The
    Dhammapada : Verses and Stories. Editorial Committee, Burma
    Tipitaka Association. Rangoon, Burma, 1986. XXIII.Nagavagga,
    Verse 327.

23. Kahneman, Daniel. Thinking, Fast and Slow. 1 ed., New York,
    Farrar, Straus And Giroux, 25 Oct. 2011, p. Part 1-Two Systems. P
    19.

24. Kahneman, Daniel. Thinking, Fast and Slow. 1 ed., New York,
    Farrar, Straus And Giroux, 25 Oct. 2011, p. Part 1-Two Systems. P
    19.

25. Ñāṇamoli, Bhikkhu, and Bhikkhu Bodhi. The Middle Length
    Discourses of the Buddha : A Translation of the Majjhima Nikāya.
    Somerville, Massachusetts, Wisdom Publications, In Association
    With The Barre Center For Buddhist Studies, 2015, p. 1039.

26. Trans. Ideal Solitude. BPS Wheel No 188, 1973.
    Translation of MN 131 with introduction and notes.
    Deepak Chopra. Buddha : A Story of Enlightenment. New York,
    Harperone, 2008, pp. 89–95.

27. Kahneman, Daniel. Thinking, Fast and Slow. 1 ed., New York, Farrar, Straus And Giroux, 25 Oct. 2011, Part 3 – Overconfidence, Chapter 21 – Intuitions vs Formulas. P 222.

28. Paul Meehl, Clinical vs. Statistical Predictions: A Theoretical Analysis and a Review of the Evidence. Minneapolis: University of Minnesota Press, 1954.

29. Kahneman, Daniel, et al. Judgment Under Uncertainty : Heuristics And Biases. Cambridge ; New York, Cambridge University Press, 1982.

30. 1985 August, The American Statistician, Volume 39, Number 3, Article: The Key Role of Statisticians in the Transformation of North American Industry, Author: Brian L. Joiner, Start Page 224, Quote Page 226, Published by Taylor & Francis, Ltd. on behalf of the American Statistical Association.

31. Huai-Nan Tzu, and Thomas F Cleary. The Book of Leadership and Strategy : Lessons of the Chinese Masters. Kindle Edition ed., Boston, Shambhala ; [New York, 1992, p. 139.

32. Harari, Yuval Noah. A Brief History of Humankind. Kinneret, Zmora-Bitan, Dvir - Publishing House Ltd, 2013, Chapter 2 – The Tree of Knowledge, p 29–47.

33. Harrison, Neil, and Dreamstime.com. "Lion-Man. Prehistoric, Paleolithic," Dreamstime.Com, www.dreamstime.com/lion-man-upper-half-majestic-oldest-piece-sculpture-existance-hohlenstein-aged-years-old-isolated-against-image125041948. Photo 125041948 © Neil Harrison.

34. Harari, Yuval Noah. A Brief History of Humankind. Kinneret, Zmora-Bitan, Dvir - Publishing House Ltd, 2013, Chapter 2 – The Tree of Knowledge, p 33.

35. "About Tesla | Tesla." Www.Tesla.Com, www.tesla.com/about. Accessed 6 June 2020.

36. Hindle, Tim. GUIDE TO MANAGEMENT IDEAS AND GURUS. THE ECONOMIST IN ASSOCIATION WITH PROFILE BOOKS LTD, 2008, p. 134.

37. "About NASA." NASA, 2020, www.nasa.gov/about/index.html.

38. Huai-Nan Tzu, and Thomas F Cleary. The Book of Leadership and Strategy : Lessons of the Chinese Masters. Kindle Edition ed., Boston, Shambhala ; [New York, 1992, p. 845.

39. Clifford, Catherine. "The Founder of Patagonia Fishes Half the Year and Tells His Employees to Go Surfing." CNBC Make It, 23 Dec. 2016, www.cnbc.com/2016/12/23/founder-of-patagonia-fishes-half-the-year-tells-his-employees-to-surf.html. Accessed 6 June 2020.

    In an interview on the NPR podcast "How I Built This":

    Chouinard, Yvon. Patagonia: Yvon Chouinard. 25 Dec. 2017, www.npr.org/2018/02/06/572558864/patagonia-yvon-chouinard. Accessed 6 June 2020.

40. Delaney, Hollie. "Zappos Gives New Employees 4 Weeks to Decide If It's a Good Fit — and Lets Them Quit with Pay If Not. Their Head of HR Explains How This Policy Has Helped Them Save Money and Hire Great People." Business Insider, 19 Nov. 2019, www.businessinsider.com/zappos-head-of-hr-four-weeks-onboarding-hire-great-people-2019-11.

41. Twitter. "Twitter University." YouTube, 2013, www.youtube.com/user/TwitterUniversity/about. Accessed 6 June 2020.

    Second source:

    Twitter. "Https://Twitter.Com/University." Twitter, Aug. 2013, twitter.com/university. Accessed 6 June 2020.

42. Huai-Nan Tzu, and Thomas F Cleary. The Book of Leadership and Strategy : Lessons of the Chinese Masters. Kindle Edition ed., Boston, Shambhala ; [New York, 1992, p. 853-854.

43. Friedrich Wilhelm Nietzsche, and Richard F H Polt. Twilight of the Idols, or, How to Philosophize with the Hammer. 1889. Indianapolis, Ind., Hackett Pub, 1997, p. 6. Epigrams and Arrows 12.

44. Maslow, A. H. "A Theory of Human Motivation." Psychological Review, vol. 50, no. 4, 1943, pp. 370–396, 10.1037/h0054346.

45. Guttmann, Philipp, and Artyl. "English: Dynamic Hierarchy of Needs of Abraham Maslow Referring to Krech, D./Crutchfield, R. S./Ballachey, E. L. (1962), Individual in Society, Tokyo Etc. 1962, S. 77." Wikimedia Commons, 16 Oct. 2016, commons.wikimedia.org/wiki/File:Dynamic_hierarchy_of_needs_-_Maslow.svg. Creative Commons Attribution-Share Alike 4.0 International license.(CC BY-SA 4.0).

46. Maslow, Abraham H, Motivation And Personality. Prabhat Prakashan, 1 Jan. 1981, p. 46.

47. Ariely, Dan. Predictably Irrational : The Hidden Forces That Shape Our Decisions. London, Harper Collins, 2008, pp. 67–88.

48. Kahneman, Daniel, and Amos Tversky. "Prospect Theory: An Analysis of Decision under Risk." Econometrica, vol. 47, no. 2, Mar. 1979, p. 263, 10.2307/1914185. Accessed 7 Dec. 2018.

49. Guttmann, Philipp, and Artyl. "English: Dynamic Hierarchy of Needs of Abraham Maslow Referring to Krech, D./Crutchfield, R. S./Ballachey, E. L. (1962), Individual in Society, Tokyo Etc. 1962, S. 77." Wikimedia Commons, 16 Oct. 2016, commons.wikimedia.org/wiki/File:Dynamic_hierarchy_of_needs_-_Maslow.svg. Creative Commons Attribution-Share Alike 4.0 International license.(CC BY-SA 4.0).

50. Without changing license, added by Ariel Feyderov a personal preference to risk illustration from figure 3-4 of this book.

51. Tzetzes, John, and Gottlieb Kiesling. Ioannou Tou Tzetzou Biblion Historikes Tes Dia Stichon Politikon. Hildesheim G. Olms, 1963, p. 46.

   Sunzi. The Art of War. Kindle ed., Mineola, N.Y., Dover Publications, 2002, p. 51.

52. Christensen, Clayton M, et al. "Reinventing Your Business Model." Harvard Business Review, vol. 2008, no. R0812C, Dec. 2008. HARVARD BUSINESS SCHOOL PUBLISHING CORPORATION.

53. Eisenhower, D.: A speech to the National Defense Executive Reserve Conference in Washington, D.C., November 14, 1957. In: Eisenhower, D. (ed.) Public Papers of the Presidents of the United States, p. 818. National Archives and Records Service, Government Printing Office (1957).

54. Philip Martin Mccaulay, and Sunzi. Sun Tzu's The Art of War. First ed., Raleigh, North Carolina, Lulu.Com, 2009, p. 35.

55. *Epicurus,* Diogenes Laertius X. P 148

56. Liu, Zhifeng, et al. "How Much of the World's Land Has Been Urbanized, Really? A Hierarchical Framework for Avoiding Confusion." Landscape Ecology, vol. 29, no. 5, 12 Apr. 2014, pp. 763–771, 10.1007/s10980-014-0034-y. Accessed 24 Feb. 2020.

57. Liu, Zhifeng, et al. "How Much of the World's Land Has Been Urbanized, Really? A Hierarchical Framework for Avoiding Confusion." Landscape Ecology, vol. 29, no. 5, 12 Apr. 2014, pp. 763–771, 10.1007/s10980-014-0034-y., FIGURE 1, P 5. Accessed 24 Feb. 2020.

58. "68% of the World Population Projected to Live in Urban Areas by 2050, Says UN | UN DESA | United Nations Department of Economic and Social Affairs." UN DESA | United Nations Department of Economic and Social Affairs, 16 May 2018, www.un.org/development/desa/en/news/population/2018-revision-of-world-urbanization-prospects.html.

59. Trombley, Stephen, and Pythagoras of Samos Greek philosopher. Wise Words : The Philosophy of Everyday Life. London, Head Of Zeus, 2017. Chapter fifteen: Friendship, quote No ii.

60. Cooper, Nancy, and NEWSWEEK EDITORS. "The Top 10 Hospitals In the World." NEWSWEEK, 3 June 20AD, p. https://www.newsweek.com/2020/03/06/top-10-hospitals-world-1489794.html, www.newsweek.com/best-hospitals-2020. Accessed 9 June 2020.

61. Nassim Nicholas Taleb. Antifragile : Things That Gain from Disorder. New York, Random House, 2012.

62. Taleb, Nassim Nicholas, and Raphaël Douady. Mathematical Definition, Mapping, and Detection of (Anti)Fragility. HAL Archives Ouvertes, Documents de Travail du Centre d'Economie de la Sorbonne, 1 Dec. 2014, p. 4, hal.archives-ouvertes.fr/hal-01151340. Accessed 11 June 2020. Figure 1.

63. Taleb, Nassim Nicholas., Philosophy: 'Antifragility' as a mathematical idea. Nature, 2013 Feb 28; 494(7438), 430-430

64. Viktor Emil Frankl. Man's Search for Meaning : An Introduction to Logotherapy. translated by ILSE LASCH, Fourth ed., Boston, Beacon Press, 1992, p. 117.

65. Conan Doyle. The Sign of the Four. A Scandal in Bohemia, and Other Stories. New York, A.L. Burt, 1920.

66. https://www.shutterstock.com/image-vector/silhouette-flat-icon-simple-vector-design-673389343

67. Green, Paul E., and V. Srinivasan. "Conjoint Analysis in Consumer Research: Issues and Outlook." Journal of Consumer Research, vol. 5, no. 2, 1978, pp. 103–123, www.jstor.org/stable/2489001. Accessed 11 June 2020.

68. Nabil Sabio Azadi., Chandler, Otis. "A Quote by Nabil Sabio Azadi." Www.Goodreads.Com, www.goodreads.com/quotes/8790564-when-fishermen-cannot-go-to-sea-they-repair-nets#:~:text=Quote%20by%20Nabil%20Sabio%20Azadi.

69. Abraham Lincoln, 1960 May, Roads and Streets, Volume 103, (Advertisement for distributor of Williams Equipment for digging), Quote Page 37, Gillette Publishing Co., Chicago, Illinois. (Verified with scans; thanks to librarian at the University of Central Florida

70. Gordon, Charles George. Sir William Francis Butler. Macmillan and Company, 1892, p. 85.

71. Aurelius, Marcus, and Gregory Hays. Meditations. NEW YORK, THE MODERN LIBRARY, 2002. Book 12, quote 4.

Made in the USA
Las Vegas, NV
28 December 2020